THE ARCHAEOLOGY OF MINOAN CRETE

A BODLEY HEAD ARCHAEOLOGY

The Archaeology of Minoan Crete

REYNOLD HIGGINS

Drawings by
ROSEMONDE NAIRAC

THE BODLEY HEAD · London Sydney Toronto

UNIFORM WITH THIS BOOK

MAGNUS MAGNUSSON *Introducing Archaeology*
T. G. H. JAMES *The Archaeology of Ancient Egypt*
RONALD HARKER *Digging up the Bible Lands*
MAGNUS MAGNUSSON *Viking Expansion Westwards*

IN PREPARATION

BARRY CUNLIFFE *Rome and the Barbarians*
PAUL JOHNSTONE *The Archaeology of Sea-faring*
HUMPHREY CASE *The Beginnings of European Civilisation*

FRONTISPIECE
The Villa of Ayia
Triada today.

TO MY PARENTS

© Reynold Higgins 1973
Drawings © The Bodley Head Ltd 1973
ISBN 0 370 01575 4
Printed and bound in Great Britain for
The Bodley Head Ltd
9 Bow Street, London WC2E 7AL
by William Clowes and Sons Ltd, Beccles
Filmset in Monophoto Ehrhardt by
BAS Printers Ltd, Wallop, Hampshire
First published 1973

CONTENTS

ACKNOWLEDGMENTS

My wife and my son Nicolas read this book in typescript and made many helpful suggestions; Mr Nicolas Coldstream did the same for Chapter 10. I am very grateful to them. Thanks are also due to the following for permission to reproduce black and white photographic material: Hirmer Verlag, Munich, frontispiece and pages 14, 59, 95, 101; Peter Clayton, pages 10, 11, 13, 19, 20, 24, 27, 36, 43, 45, 46, 51, 58, 62, 66, 69, 100; Department of Antiquities, Ashmolean Museum, Oxford, pages 17, 21, 28, 37, 39, 40, 44, 50, 54, 94, 98, 99; Josephine Powell, pages 22, 23, 47, 63, 68; the Trustees of the British Museum, pages 26, 29, 34 (*top*), 103, 104; Keith Branigan, page 33; Dr Peter Warren, pages 34 (*bottom*) and 35; Leonard von Matt, Buochs, Switzerland, pages 52, 56, 72, 75, 82; Professor Nicolas Platon, page 76; the late Dr Gisela M.A. Richter, page 79; Pennsylvania University Museum, Philadelphia, page 84; Professor G. Huxley and Nicolas Coldstream, page 87; Professor J. Luce, pages 88 and 91; Mrs Lois Ventris, page 105. Thanks for permission to use coloured photographic material are due to Professor Spiridon Marinatos, Inspector General of the Archaeological Services of Greece, jacket and facing page 81; Hirmer Verlag, Munich, for the two photographs facing page 32; Ekdotike Athenon of Athens for a photograph from their *History of the Hellenic World*, Volume I, facing page 33; Peter Clayton, facing pages 49, 64, and 80 (*top and bottom left*); Leonard von Matt, facing page 48, Josephine Powell, facing page 65; the Trustees of the British Museum, facing page 80 (*bottom right*).

In addition I am grateful to the following for permission to quote copyright material: the editors of *Archaeology*, The Archaeological Institute of America, for extracts from *Memoirs of a Pioneer Excavator in Crete* by Harriet Boyd Hawes, from vol. XVIII (1965) on pages 79–81, 83 and 85, the Agathon Press Inc, New York, for extracts from *The Palace of Minos* by Sir Arthur Evans on pages 42–46 and 49. Professor Walter Graham kindly allowed the drawings on pages 16 and 70 to be based on reconstructions which appeared in his *Palaces of Crete*; the drawings on pages 32 and 73 are based on ones which appeared in *The Minoans* by Sinclair Hood published by Thames & Hudson Ltd; and the drawing on page 86 is based on a photograph supplied by Nicolas Coldstream.

INTRODUCTION

'Out in the dark blue sea there lies a land called Crete, a rich and lovely land, washed by waves on every side, densely peopled and boasting ninety cities. Each of the several races of the isle has its own language . . . One of the ninety towns is a great city called Knossos, and there, for nine years, King Minos ruled and enjoyed the friendship of almighty Zeus.'

Thus, in Homer's *Odyssey*, Odysseus the wanderer described to his wife Penelope the largest of the Greek islands. Crete lies to the south-east of the Greek mainland, almost equidistant from Europe, Asia and Africa. It is long, narrow and very mountainous, measuring some 150 miles from east to west and, on average, some twenty miles from north to south; and along the whole length of the island runs a high spine reaching up to 8000 feet at the summit of Mount Ida in the centre.

A modern traveller would hardly recognise Crete from Homer's description, although physically it has not changed very much. The highlands have never been good for anything but grazing sheep and goats, but the lowlands have always been, by Greek standards, fertile, yielding cereals, beans, olives, and grapes. The principal difference is that Crete was much more heavily wooded in ancient times than it is today, and the citrus fruits and bananas which grow there now so abundantly were unknown in antiquity. But the climate is still almost perfect, with mild sunny winters and hot summers tempered by cooling sea breezes.

Modern Crete, then, is still a 'rich and lovely land, washed by waves on every side'. But a hundred years ago, no one believed the

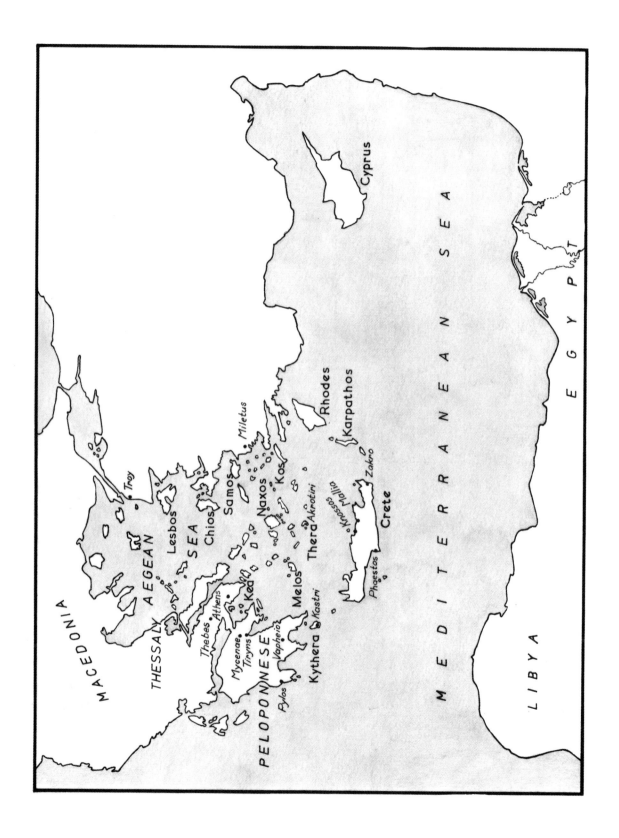

rest of Homer's description: 'densely peopled and boasting ninety cities'. For the ancient civilisation that Homer described had been totally forgotten.

Yet today we know beyond doubt that the history of Crete stretches for thousands of years back into the past. We know that it had palaces and great cities. Indeed, some four or five thousand years ago, Crete was the centre of the earliest known European civilisation, equalling those of Babylonia and Egypt.

Around 1100 BC this brilliant world came to a sudden end, struck down by disasters whose nature we do not fully understand, and vanished almost without a trace. And so, by the time Homer was writing in the eighth century BC, and even more when history began to be written in Greece in the fifth century BC, memories of that civilisation had grown very dim and the stories associated with early Crete are more like fairy tales than sober fact.

Almost the only names that had come down through the centuries were those of King Minos and his capital city of Knossos; and the historians remembered him chiefly as a sea-king, the ruler of the first major naval power in the Mediterranean. The Greek historian Thucydides wrote in the fifth century BC:

'Minos is the earliest ruler we know of who possessed a fleet, and controlled most of what are now Greek waters. He ruled the Cyclades, and was the first coloniser of most of them, installing his own sons as governors. In all probability he cleared the sea of pirates, so far as he could, to secure his own revenues.'

There were a number of legends about King Minos and Crete, and some of them were contradictory. According to one story, Minos was the son of Zeus himself, who had been born in a cave on Crete; Minos's mother was Europa, whom Zeus had wooed in the shape of a bull and taken to Crete. With this divine parentage Minos was seen as a great law-giver, and it was said that he had gone to the sacred cave of Zeus for inspiration, and emerged with a code of laws—as Moses had on Mount Sinai.

But other stories stressed a more sinister side to his personality, and this aspect is enshrined in the legend of Theseus and the Minotaur. It was said that under the Palace of Knossos there was a labyrinth, or maze, and that in it lived a fearful monster, half-man and half-bull, the Minotaur, who was the offspring of a bull and Minos's wife, Pasiphae. This labyrinth had been constructed by the king's chief craftsman, Daedalus, in such an intricate way that no

The Eastern
Mediterranean

9

one who entered the maze had any hope of finding his way out again. Minos had conquered Athens with his navy; and as tribute from the defeated city he demanded that the Athenians should send to Crete every year twelve Athenian youths and maidens to be devoured by the Minotaur.

Then one year the hero Theseus, prince of Athens, volunteered to go as one of the sacrificial group. Minos's daughter, Ariadne, fell in love with him, and rather than see him die she made a plan with the aid of Daedalus to help him escape from the labyrinth after killing the Minotaur. Ariadne gave Theseus a ball of thread, which Theseus fastened to the door of the labyrinth as he went in and paid out as he set off in search of the Minotaur. After a battle in which he killed the Minotaur, he was able to retrace his steps to safety by following the thread back to the door.

Ariadne then fled from Crete with Theseus. But Daedalus stayed behind, and soon King Minos realised that his chief craftsman had betrayed him so he imprisoned Daedalus and his son Icarus to stop them leaving Crete. Daedalus was a brilliant engineer, and he devised an ingenious method of escape. He constructed a pair of feathered wings for himself, and another for his son, and together they flew off across the sea. Daedalus had warned his son not to fly too high, but Icarus was intoxicated by the sensation of flying and disregarded his father's warning. Higher and higher he flew, trying to reach the sun, until the heat of the sun melted the wax that held the wings together and Icarus plunged to his death in the ocean. Daedalus himself reached Sicily safely; and when the vengeful King Minos followed him there, Minos was mysteriously murdered, and went down to Hades to become one of the judges of the dead.

It was against this fairy-tale background that archaeology began

Cretans bringing offerings to an Egyptian official, Rekhmire. Fresco from his tomb at Thebes, *c.* 1450 BC.

The north entrance of the Palace at Knossos today.

to piece together the true story of early Crete. Archaeology is in fact the only reliable source for our knowledge of these ancient times, apart from a very few references in contemporary Egyptian or Asiatic records and those inscriptions in Cretan writing which have so far been deciphered. As a science, archaeology is scarcely a hundred years old, and the archaeology of Crete is even younger, dating back only to about 1900. But information is accumulating rapidly; and our knowledge, although not yet history in the true sense of the word, is getting pretty close to it.

How can historical dates be put to events that happened before the beginning of written history? There are two methods. The first, which has been practised for a considerable time, consists of cross-references with regions whose history is firmly established. Thus, when Cretan objects are found in Egypt or Western Asia, it is frequently possible to date them from the objects with which they were found; and conversely, Egyptian or Western Asiatic objects imported into Crete can often give a date to the archaeological levels in which they are found.

The second method is comparatively new. It is a by-product of atomic physics, and consists of measuring the amount of radioactive carbon, or Carbon 14, in selected samples of dead organic material. This scientific method, known as radiocarbon dating, can give at least approximate dates, to within a century or two, of when the organism died—wood, or bone, or plant remains, and so on.

But even with the aid of sophisticated modern techniques, many problems about Crete remain unsolved, or at least are still in dispute. All the dates given in this book have to be approximate, and I have also made two basic assumptions: I accept the decipherment by the late Michael Ventris of the Cretan script called Linear B and its identification as a basically *Greek* language (see Chapter 13), and I would date the fall of Knossos around 1400 BC, as most scholars agree, and not, as Professor L. R. Palmer argues, around 1150 BC.

1

The Early History of Crete

The first known inhabitants of Crete belonged to the Neolithic Period, or New Stone Age, when tools and weapons were still made of stone and metalwork was as yet unknown. They arrived about 6000 BC from somewhere in Western Asia—we cannot say exactly where—and settled at a number of places in Crete. Archaeological evidence of their occupation has been found at Knossos and elsewhere.

These early settlers were peasant farmers who cultivated crops and bred cattle, sheep, and goats. Their houses were largely of mud brick with flat roofs. In the very earliest times it appears that they did not even know how to make pottery, but they were soon producing a dark burnished ware with white-filled incisions and ornamental excrescences. The pottery was all hand-made, for the potter's wheel was not introduced until much later.

Their weapons and tools were frequently made of obsidian, a natural volcanic glass imported from the island of Melos. They spun and wove cloth, and made crude female idols of fired clay (terracotta) which they probably worshipped as representations of their goddess.

After a slow and peaceful development over some 3000 years the first Cretans were reinforced by new arrivals from Asia Minor, who brought with them the revolutionary arts of metalworking, in copper, bronze (an alloy of copper and tin), silver, and gold. This new civilisation, which had evolved in the Middle East at a very early date and gradually spread over Western Asia and Europe, is known generally as the Bronze Age, from the metal used for making tools and weapons.

In Crete this Bronze Age civilisation flourished for some two thousand years with especial brilliance, and was given a name by

Neolithic terracotta goddess from Knossos, *c.* 4000 BC.

13

A Neolithic cup from Knossos, c. 4000 BC.

one of the earliest and most celebrated pioneers of Cretan archaeology, Sir Arthur Evans, the excavator of Knossos. He called it 'Minoan', after that legendary ruler of Knossos, King Minos. It has been objected that it is scarcely reasonable to name a whole civilisation after one king, and the last of his line at that, but Evans believed that 'Minos' was not a personal name but a royal title, like the Egyptian Pharaoh, and he may well have been right.

Cretan potters were restless and inventive craftsmen and were never content to keep to the same style of pottery for long; they were constantly changing the shapes and the styles of decoration. Sir Arthur Evans used the different pottery styles he found at Knossos to create a framework for the chronology of Minoan history. He divided the Minoan Age into three main periods, which he called Early, Middle, and Late Minoan (usually abbreviated to EM, MM, and LM), and which corresponded in a general way with the Old, Middle, and New Kingdoms of Egypt. These periods were each sub-divided into three stages, indicated by Roman numerals, so that we get EM II, MM III, LM I, and so on. The dates which Evans assigned to these periods, based largely on cross-references with Egypt, have proved surprisingly accurate, but the language has always appeared rather confusing to the layman.

This classification into Minoan periods has never been entirely satisfactory to the expert either, and recently the Greek archaeologist Nicolas Platon has devised an alternative system, which is adopted in this book, based not on pottery styles but on architectural and cultural developments in the palaces—'Palatial' rather than 'Minoan'. Platon divided the Cretan Bronze Age into four periods, not three:

14

Pre-palatial (before any palaces were built), First-palatial (the period of the first palaces), Second-palatial (the period of the second palaces which replaced the first), and Post-palatial (the period after the destruction of the last surviving palace, at Knossos).

This new classification can be summarised, side by side with that of Evans, as follows:

Platon	Approximate Dates	Evans
Pre-palatial	3000—2000 BC	Early Minoan
First-palatial	2000—1700 BC	Middle Minoan I & II
Second-palatial	1700—1400 BC	$\begin{cases} \text{Middle Minoan III} \\ \text{Late Minoan I \& II} \end{cases}$
Post-palatial	1400—1100 BC	Late Minoan III

The Pre-palatial period lasted for about a thousand years, during which rapid strides were made in art and technology. It ended, gradually and peacefully, about 2000 BC, when palaces sprang up at Knossos, Phaestos, Mallia, and Zakro, and probably at other as yet undiscovered sites. Court life gave a tremendous impetus to Cretan artists and craftsmen, who produced triumphs of metalworking, seal-engraving, pottery and other arts.

But around 1700 BC, while at the height of their prosperity, all the known Cretan palaces were destroyed by a violent earthquake. The disaster was quickly overcome, however, and the palaces were immediately rebuilt on an even grander scale, to usher in the Second-palatial period.

Cretan culture now spread outwards. It spread to the Cycladic islands, where we can see it especially clearly on the island of Thera, or Santorini as it is known today. It even spread as far as the Greek mainland, especially Mycenae, where it combined with the local culture there to form the famous Mycenaean civilisation which Homer echoes so vividly in the *Iliad* and which the celebrated German archaeologist Heinrich Schliemann rediscovered in the nineteenth century.

Life in the Cretan palaces in the Second-palatial period was even more artistic and luxurious than before; goldsmiths, silversmiths, bronze-workers, ivory-workers, seal-engravers, faience-workers, fresco-painters and potters worked for the local rulers to create a culture of a standard which had never been attained before in Greek lands and which would not be seen again for many centuries. The palaces themselves were built by architects and engineers and craftsmen of such skill that the idea of a genius like Daedalus does not seem out of place.

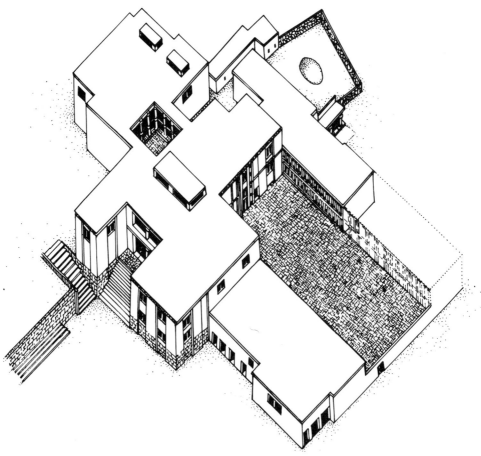

A conjectural restoration of the Palace at Phaestos. The general plan and style are typical of Minoan palatial architecture

Then disaster struck again. About 1450 BC, after a mere two and a half centuries, these flourishing palaces and the smaller settlements were destroyed. In most instances there is evidence that the damage was done by fire, but some buildings also seem to have been affected by earthquakes, and even by floods. This time there was no rebuilding; with the temporary exception of Knossos the ruined palaces were abandoned for ever.

Scholars are still arguing about the cause of this destruction. It used to be thought that the damage was done by an invading army, but the most prevalent view now is that the fires were started by earthquakes connected with a terrible volcanic eruption on the island of Santorini accompanied by falls of poisonous volcanic ash which made the eastern half of Crete uninhabitable for a number of years.

So the Second-palatial period ended probably in some natural catastrophe. Of the palaces, only Knossos survived the cataclysm

16

sufficiently intact to be worth repairing. But now, it seems, Knossos was occupied by foreigners—Mycenaeans from the Greek mainland, who presumably saw an opportunity of moving in while Crete was devastated and defenceless and who gradually extended their dominion over all Crete from this stronghold.

Their rule, however, was short, for soon after 1400 BC their palace at Knossos was burnt down, never to be rebuilt. Opinions are divided as to the cause of this fresh disaster, but the most likely theory is that it was a rebellion by the native Cretans against their alien Mycenaean overlords.

The leadership in this part of the world had now passed from Crete to Mycenae. Crete was henceforth a second-rate power; it was a member of the so-called Mycenaean Empire, but it preferred to take no part in power politics and to continue in the old ways as far as its reduced circumstances would permit.

Seal and impression showing a galloping stag from Rethymnon of about 1700 BC

For some two centuries life in Crete went on relatively peacefully and uneventfully. Then about 1200 BC new parties of Mycenaean Greeks began to arrive, refugees from serious troubles in their own homeland. A hybrid culture arose in Crete which might have developed into something of real artistic merit, but this too was extinguished about 1100 BC by the arrival from Greece of yet another wave of invaders.

These were the Dorian Greeks, and it was they who finally put an end to what was left of the 2000-year-old Bronze Age Minoan civilisation. The Dorians were a branch of the Greek family which had previously lived outside and to the north of the Mycenaean world. It is not known whether they were pushed southwards by people pressing on their northern borders, or whether they just wanted to share in the good things of the Mycenaean world; but around 1100 BC they seem to have poured into Greece in such strength as to extinguish the Mycenaean culture already weakened by earlier disasters.

These events left the Greek world so weak and so poor that for over two hundred years the people possessed only the bare necessities of life, and had no commercial contact with the civilisations of Western Asia and Egypt. Then a slow recovery started, which was to end in the great classical civilisation of Greece of the sixth to the fourth centuries BC. But by then the splendour of Minoan Crete had faded into oblivion.

17

2

Life in Minoan Crete

What was life like in Crete in the great days of the sixteenth and fifteenth centuries BC? We know quite a lot about the daily life of the Cretans, even though we are not so fortunate as those who study ancient Egypt, for many everyday objects which survive in the dry air of Egypt quickly rot in the damper Cretan climate. For example, archaeologists have to make do without the textiles and leather of which their clothes were made; the wood of which much of their houses and all their furniture was made; and the papyrus which they probably used for writing on. They have to rely on paintings; on objects of metal, pottery and faience; on carved stone and ivory; and on their own common sense.

Royalty and the royal households lived in palaces of several storeys with large airy rooms, grouped round a central court. As is usual in this part of the world to this day, the roofs were always flat. There was a piped water supply, built-in drainage, flushing water-closets and fixed terracotta baths. The rooms had plastered walls which were often decorated with colourful frescoes.

The rich inhabited luxurious country mansions which were smaller and simpler versions of the palaces. How the poor lived we do not know, since their houses were too flimsy to have survived.

A Minoan palace was much more than a royal residence. It was also the seat of government and a religious centre, for the king seems also to have been a sort of High Priest. In addition, the palace contained workshops, armouries, and stores and provisions for much of the entire kingdom. Food, especially olive oil and grain, was kept in enormous barrel-shaped jars of pottery, some as high as a man. The tradition of making such huge jars persists in Crete to this day.

Minoan food was pretty well what it is today. For meat there was pork, mutton and goat. Beef was rare, as it is now, for the Cretan countryside is not really suitable for cattle. It was, however, rich in wild game: deer, wild boar, hares, ducks, geese and partridges. Fish was popular too, and was plentiful, as it always has been until the recent destructive custom of fishing with dynamite. It included shellfish and octopuses, which are still regarded as a great delicacy.

Bread was made from wheat or barley, and was probably unleavened like modern Arab bread. There was also milk (from sheep and goats) and cheese; but no butter.

Fruit was abundant, especially apples, pears, grapes, pomegranates, figs and dates; and there were several kinds of nuts. For vegetables there were peas and lentils; and there was the all-important olive, whose oil was, and still is, a vital part of the diet in these regions. Honey was used for sweetening, for sugar was not yet known. The principal drink was wine, but the Cretans probably also made 'tea' from the various herbs which grow so freely in Crete.

Fixed hearths were very rare, and the cooking seems to have been done over portable charcoal braziers. Numbers of enormous copper cooking-pots have been found in the palaces and big houses, but ordinary folk used plain pottery. The fine table-ware was also of pottery. It consisted of drinking-cups (made either like modern tea-cups or modern wine-glasses), bowls, jugs for wine, and jars.

Terracotta bathtub which was subsequently used as a coffin.

19

Some of the large storage jars in the West Magazines at Knossos.

The favourite storage-jar for liquids was the so-called stirrup-jar, which had a false spout on top with a strap-handle on either side and a genuine spout beside it. They vary in size from a few inches to several feet in height.

The women wore long flounced dresses with a tight-waisted short-sleeved bodice which left the breasts bare. These dresses often had patterns made from thin gold leaf sewn to them. Their hair was elaborately dressed, and they wore beads of gold or blue glass round their necks and their wrists.

20

Men wore a loin-cloth or kilt, a tight belt, and high leather boots to protect their feet and legs from the prickly undergrowth. They did not as a rule wear jewellery, except for a gold signet ring on one finger, or a stone seal on a cord round the wrist. Seals and signets were used to put the owner's personal mark on documents or bundles of goods or jars of provisions; the seals were pressed into the wet clay that was attached to the string of the bundle or to the mouth of the jar. The seals were exquisitely carved with religious scenes or studies of people or animals. The stones—rock crystal, amethyst, jasper, lapis lazuli and haematite—were chosen for their beauty, and were carved by means of a drill and an engraving tool.

Religion for the Cretans was a happy affair, and was celebrated in palace-shrines, or else in open-air sanctuaries on the tops of mountains and in sacred caves. They worshipped a mother-goddess and a young god, probably her son, and sacrificed bulls to them.

Seal and its impression of a prancing bitch of about 1500 BC.

Their religion was closely bound up with their recreations. First in importance were the bull-sports, which probably took place in the central courts of the palaces. Young men and women working in teams would take it in turn to grasp the horns of a charging bull and somersault over its back: a dangerous sport, which doubtless saw many casualties. It may well have survived down to the present day, as in the Landes district of France where young men turn somersaults over charging cows.

Boxing and wrestling were also practised by the young men of Crete. In one scene on a relief-vase the boxers appear to be wearing knuckledusters. Another relief-vase shows a rustic spring festival, with singing and dancing to the accompaniment of a sistrum, a rattle-like instrument of Egyptian origin. One popular dance was like the dances still to be seen in Greece today, in which the performers stand in a circle and dance with linked arms.

Dancing and singing were usually given a musical accompaniment on the lyre or the double-pipes, or both. The nature of the music of the double-pipes is not clear; all we know is that the player had two pipes in his mouth and played them both at the same time, holding one in each hand and blocking the stops with his fingers.

Art, too, was closely connected with religion. Minoan artists are remarkable for the excellence of their workmanship, for their incredible vitality, for their skill in portraying the world of nature—animals, birds, trees and flowers—and for their ability to reproduce movement in a snapshot-like impressionistic way. They usually preferred to work on a small scale, and their best products are ivory-

Two gold cups with embossed scenes showing the capture of bulls for the bull-sports, from Vapheio near Sparta, *c.* 1450 BC. About three and a half inches tall.

carvings, small bronze figures, engraved gems and gold jewellery.

Another small-scale art at which they excelled was in the making of stone vases. At all periods they made simple but graceful shapes from veined and mottled stones. In addition, in the fifteenth century BC, they also carved scenes in relief on vases of soft stone and then plated them with gold. In doing this they were obviously imitating true gold vases. Relief-vases in gold have not yet been found in Crete, but a pair of cups from a tomb at Vapheio in South Greece, near Sparta, was made in Crete and imported by a Mycenaean king of Sparta. They are a matching pair with a common theme, the catching of wild bulls for the bull-sports. On one the animal is being caught in a net, in a scene of wild confusion: on the other it is being lured into captivity by a decoy cow. Seldom have animals been shown with greater realism.

As jewellers the Cretans were beyond compare. By 2000 BC they had mastered almost every aspect of this craft: relief-work, inlay, filigree, granulation (decoration by means of minute balls of gold), and the making of delicate chains.

22

Almost their only large-scale works are the wall-paintings of the palaces, which give us a vivid glimpse of palace life, of religion, of sport, and country scenery.

Of course, they learned much from abroad. They were in contact with the Hittites of Asia Minor, with Syria and with Egypt. Indeed some of the finest Egyptian tomb-paintings of the fifteenth century BC show Cretans bringing vases and statuettes of gold and silver as offerings. But they never copied other people's artistic ideas; they preferred to adapt them to their own needs.

Burial customs were different at different times, but the Cretans always buried their dead unburnt, and usually put in the grave some of the dead person's possessions, for use in the next world: pottery and seals for both sexes, a man's weapons and a woman's jewellery. The body was trussed tight in a crouching position, knees to chin, and was either laid on the floor of the tomb or crammed into a jar.

In the early times, down to about 1600 BC, they preferred round stone tombs, probably roofed with timber, for communal burial. One such tomb might have several hundreds of burials in it.

23

Occasionally, however, communal tombs were built more like houses, on a rectangular plan.

From 1600 BC it was more usual to bury the dead in small tombs, called chamber-tombs, cut into the soft rock of the hillsides, and intended only for two or three occupants. They were usually placed in terracotta bath-tubs or in terracotta coffins imitating wooden clothes chests.

After the arrival of the Mycenaeans at Knossos about 1450 BC, the Mycenaean 'beehive' tomb was occasionally used for royal burials. This sort of tomb was a development by Mycenaean architects of the early Cretan communal round tomb, adapted for a king and his immediate family, and reintroduced into Crete by the conquerors. The tomb is approached by a stone-built passage cut into the hillside. The chamber at the end of the passage is the shape of a beehive, lined with carefully cut blocks of stone.

It is not known what language the early Cretans spoke before the arrival of the Greeks about 1450 BC—only that it was not Greek. A number of Cretan words, however, were taken over by the Greeks, and some have even survived to our own day, such as 'hyacinth', 'terebinth' (turpentine) and 'cypress'. It seems clear from the comparative rarity of pre-Greek inscriptions that the knowledge of writing in Crete before 1450 BC was confined to a small class of scribes, and that the mass of the population was illiterate.

A Minoan burial. The body was trussed tight in a crouching position.

24

3

Aftermath and Rediscovery

After the fall of the great Cretan Bronze Age civilisation Crete remained a prosperous part of the successive Greek and Roman worlds, but it never became pre-eminent again. Because they were always a bit different, the Cretans were never popular with their neighbours. St Paul, quoting an old slander, called them 'liars, evil beasts, slow bellies'. Crete continued to prosper until the Saracens captured the island in 823 and held it until 961. After further vicissitudes it was recaptured by the Crusaders, and in 1210 it was allotted to Venice, and remained, fairly happily, in Venetian hands until captured by the Turks in 1669. Turkish rule, which was to last for over two centuries, was harsh and oppressive, and under it the Cretans were poorer and more wretched than at any other time in their history.

When the Greek War of Independence broke out in 1821, the Cretans stepped up their resistance to Turkish oppression by a series of rebellions. In 1897 the Turks, while trying to put down one such rebellion, embarked on a general massacre in Candia (the early name of Heraklion), and among the victims were the British Vice-Consul and seventeen British sailors. The British admiral in charge of a squadron in the harbour thereupon trained his guns on the city and gave the Turks ten minutes to surrender, which they did. The following year the last Turkish troops left the island, the Cretans gained their freedom, and Prince George of Greece became High Commissioner of an independent Crete. Finally, in 1913, Crete was united with the kingdom of Greece.

Under the Turkish occupation very little archaeological activity had been possible; the authorities were obstructive, communications

CANDIA

A print of Candia, now Heraklion, when it was in Venetian hands in about AD 1600.

were virtually non-existent, and there was always the risk of death from disease or bandits. A few intrepid travellers, such as the Englishmen Robert Pashley and Captain (later Admiral) T. A. B. Spratt, had succeeded in identifying a number of classical sites, but the Bronze Age was completely undiscovered and unsuspected.

Robert Pashley, a Fellow of Trinity College, Cambridge, published his researches into the classical sites in a book called *Travels in Crete* in 1837. Captain Spratt (*Travels and Researches in Crete*, 1865), surveyed the coast of Crete for the British Admiralty from 1851 to 1853, and made several journeys inland, noting the archaeological remains and the geology and natural history of the island. He was assisted by his pilot, a former pirate with a detailed knowledge of the Cretan coastline.

Towards the end of Turkish rule things became somewhat easier. In 1878 the Sultan gave permission to a local archaeologist, Joseph Hazzidakis, to found a 'Society for the Promotion of Education', whose aims included the preservation of ancient monuments and the foundation of a museum in Heraklion. The museum was stocked with chance finds brought in by peasants and with gifts by private collectors. In the same year an antiquarian from Heraklion, Minos Kalokairinos, identified the site of the ancient Palace of Knossos when he excavated some store-rooms in the mound of Kefala not far from the city.

Italian interest in Cretan archaeology was started by the near-legendary Italian scholar, Federico Halbherr, a romantic figure who used to gallop over the mountains on a black Arab mare. He arrived in 1884 and, frequently in the company of Hazzidakis, prospected for ancient sites. The first recorded discovery of Bronze Age antiquities came in 1885 when Halbherr and Hazzidakis visited a

26

cave at Psychro high up the mountain of Lasithi in central Crete, and there they recovered a number of Minoan objects which the local peasants had found there. The next year the chance discovery of a ruined tomb near Phaestos was to lead to the identification of the Palace of Phaestos. And in the early 1890s the new museum at Heraklion acquired some two dozen gaily decorated vases from the Kamares Cave on Mount Ida.

The origins of this 'Kamares ware', as it was called, with its abstract designs in white, yellow and red on a black ground, were quite unknown. But in 1894, Arthur Evans paid his first visit to Crete and published a paper in which he maintained that this pottery 'overlaps the more purely Mycenaean pottery in the island'. This would suggest that it was made rather before 1600 BC. So Evans was on the right track: he had begun to suspect that there had been a civilisation on Crete earlier than the civilisation of Mycenae.

Evans's interest in Crete had begun in Athens, where he had met the archaeologist Heinrich Schliemann and become interested in Mycenaean seals. In an antique dealer's shop he found some seals of the same general kind, which puzzled him greatly. He was extremely short-sighted, and with the naked eye he could see that the seals were engraved with what seemed to be hieroglyphic writing. The dealer said the seals came from Crete; and so, in 1894, Evans went to Crete in search of more of this prehistoric writing.

In his travels he was able to buy a large number of seals from the local peasants, whose womenfolk wore them as milk-charms— amulets to ensure a plentiful supply of mother's milk; and many of these seals were engraved with the strange hieroglyphic markings. Evans was sure they were not Egyptian in origin; he saw them as evidence of some ancient form of European writing, much older

Kamares cups, named after the cave where they were first found in the early 1890s.

27

Arthur Evans at Knossos in the early days of his excavation there.

than anything known before. He was also convinced that archaeological excavation would provide confirmation of his theory.

The obvious place to dig was at Knossos. Schliemann had already tried to buy the site for excavation a few years earlier, but had failed. Evans, too, met nothing but obstruction at first, but after the declaration of Cretan independence in 1898 the obstacles were removed. Evans was able to buy the site, and in 1900 he started digging; it was to be a more formidable task than he had suspected.

Many other foreign archaeologists were equally anxious to excavate in Crete as they had been doing in Greece for some time. The more important Western European countries and the United States already had institutions in Athens where scholars could stay

28

to study the antiquities of Greece and to make excavations. Each country was allowed a limited number of excavations, usually three in any one year, at certain sites which had been allotted to them. As a general rule, all the finds from these excavations became the property of the Greek government and could not be taken away. This was in order to prevent the wholesale removal of Greek antiquities to other countries which had taken place in the past.

These institutions were known as 'schools', and the English one was known in full as the 'British School of Archaeology at Athens', usually shortened to the 'British School at Athens'. It possessed spacious premises in what was then the countryside on the lower slopes of Mount Lykabettus, and it is still the headquarters for British research and excavation in Greece.

The Director of the British School at this time was D. G. Hogarth, a friend of Arthur Evans and a keen student of early Crete. Hogarth now obtained permission to excavate at the Psychro Cave on Mount Lasithi in Central Crete, where Halbherr and Hazzidakis had found Minoan objects in 1885, and also at Zakro and Palaikastro in the east. American expeditions were active at Gournia, Vasiliki, Mochlos and other eastern sites. In the south the Italians started work in 1900 at Phaestos, where the site of a palace had just been identified. Also in the south, the Cretan archaeologist Stephanos Xanthoudides explored a number of collective burials in the Mesara Plain, starting in 1904 and continuing until 1918. A third palace, at Mallia on the north coast, was identified by Hazzidakis in 1915 and was dug by French archaeologists after the First World War.

Work also continued at Knossos after the First World War, but on the whole, interest in Minoan archaeology had now waned. There was, however, a revival just before the Second World War when the British, under John Pendlebury, conducted a survey of the Lasithi Plain and cleared a hill-city at Karphi.

After the Second World War Crete saw a tremendous resurgence of activity. The British immediately returned to Knossos, and have been excavating there on and off ever since. They have also excavated again at Palaikastro and at two sites near Myrtos in the south. The Italians have been active at Phaestos and the French at Mallia.

Stylianos Alexiou of the Greek Archaeological Service has cleared an important group of Pre-palatial circular tombs at Lebena, and his colleague John Sakellarakis uncovered at Archanes near Knossos an intact Minoan royal burial. In addition, an Anglo-American team has excavated a Minoan colony on the island of Kythera. But by far

Impressions from a four-sided Minoan hieroglyphic seal, the sort that Arthur Evans was collecting in Crete.

29

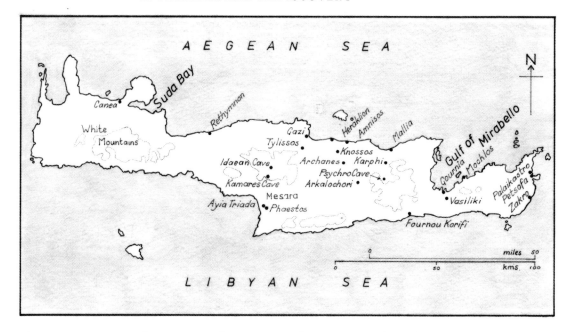

Principal excavation sites of Minoan Crete

the two most important Minoan excavations since the war have been at Zakro, on the east coast of Crete, and on the island of Santorini (ancient Thera), sixty miles to the north of Crete.

At Zakro, Nicolas Platon started digging in 1961 and has uncovered a fourth Minoan palace which had remained completely undisturbed from the time of its destruction around 1450 BC.

On Santorini, Spiridon Marinatos, Inspector General of the Greek Archaeological Service, has been excavating since 1967 a city buried under volcanic ash when the island erupted around 1500 BC —a Minoan Pompeii in effect. There are years, perhaps decades, of work to be done there yet, but already it is providing a vivid picture of life in a Minoan outpost at the height of the Bronze Age civilisation.

4

Pre-palatial Sites: the First Minoans

In the autumn of 1904 a peasant from the little village of Koumasa, in the rich Mesara Plain in the south of Crete, brought a handful of objects in to the museum at Heraklion. This chance find was to throw light on the earliest days of Minoan civilisation—the Pre-palatial period which ran from about 3000 to 2000 BC. Most of our information about this Pre-palatial period comes from a group of circular communal tombs in the Mesara Plain, and it was the peasant from Koumasa who pointed the way to their discovery.

The Cretan archaeologist Stephanos Xanthoudides was assigned the task of assessing the objects the peasant had brought. He described them later in his book, *The Vaulted Tombs of Mesara*:

'The objects, three seals, two of ivory and one of steatite, some crystal and steatite necklace beads, and some pieces of a bronze dagger with its pommel of chalcedony, were at once recognised as Early Minoan sepulchral gear . . . and were bought by the museum.

'An immediate exploration of the spot by the Archaeological Service was decided upon, since the villager said that more things had been found, vases of clay and stone and fragments of daggers, and it was to be feared that the people of the village would go on with their unauthorised digging now that they had discovered that these things had value.

'Thus it came about that in December 1904 I discovered and partly excavated the Koumasa group of tombs, four in all . . .'

Altogether, Xanthoudides dug fifteen such tombs during the next fourteen years. After his last discovery in 1918 there was a lull, and

31

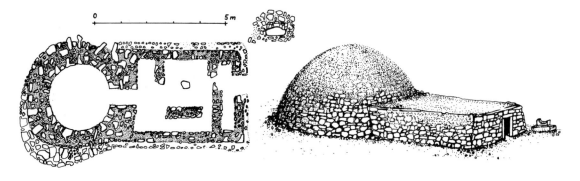

A ground plan and reconstruction of a typical Mesara Tomb

no more tombs were discovered till the mid-1950s, when Greek archaeologists returned to the search and met with considerable success. About eighty are now known, almost all in the Mesara Plain.

All the evidence relating to these Pre-palatial tombs has recently been surveyed by a young English scholar, Keith Branigan. Most of them, he concludes, were built between 3000 and 2000 BC, but many continued in use during the life of the first palaces. The tomb itself was a circular building on ground level entered by a low doorway, and varied in diameter from eight to forty feet; the average is about twenty feet. There has been much argument as to whether such buildings were originally roofed, and if so, how; Branigan believes that most of them were probably roofed with wood, while some of the latest to be built were perhaps fully vaulted in stone.

Grave-goods of many kinds were found in these tombs; nearly all would seem to have been the personal possessions of the dead when they were alive, and not to have been made specially for burial. They include pottery, terracotta figures, bronze tools and weapons, marble figures of women, stone vases, and ivory seals. The seals were commonest. The actual signets were made in many forms, frequently as figures of birds and animals, whilst the patterns engraved on them were mostly geometrical figures, often of considerable complexity.

These tombs were used over many centuries by the members of one particular clan, and one tomb could accommodate several hundred corpses in the principal chamber and in annexes built outside. The dead were trussed in the position of an unborn child, to indicate a return to the womb of Mother Earth, and were accompanied by their few personal possessions, which they would need in the next world as they did in this. When there was no longer any room on the floor of the tomb, a layer of earth was spread over the existing deposits and the burials continued on top of them.

OPPOSITE Stone vases of about 2200 BC from Mochlos. *Below* Kamares jar of about 1800 BC from Knossos.

32

An artist's reconstruction of the State Apartments in the Palace at Knossos.

Some of the best work in East Crete was done in the early 1900s by Richard Seager, a brilliant American archaeologist and friend of Arthur Evans. In 1904 and 1906 he dug a settlement near the modern village of Vasiliki, which provided important evidence for the chronology of ancient Crete. At Vasiliki Seager found the remains of a mansion so grand that it might well have been the model for the palaces which came later. But he also found a great deal of pottery from which it was possible to work out the development of patterns and shapes of pots in Crete in the period before the palaces were built, because the pottery was 'stratified'—that is to say it was found in layers corresponding to the successive periods in which it was deposited in the earth.

All the pottery of this period is hand-made, for the true potter's wheel did not come in till the period of the early palaces. But these early potters seem to have used circular turntables which they slowly rotated as they built up the pot on them.

The earliest pots are rather clumsy: round-bottomed jugs and bulbous jars decorated with simple linear patterns in a red or brown semi-lustrous paint. This paint is an early form of the so-called 'black glaze' of classical Greek pottery. It is not a true glaze but a highly refined iron-rich clay, which under oxidising conditions

The interior of a circular, communal Mesara-type tomb.

33

Vasiliki ware 'tea pot', *c*. 2500 BC. It is about four and a half inches high.

Terracotta turntables from Fournou Korifi—possibly the ancestors of the potter's wheel. Each is about nine inches in diameter.

(in a clear fire) will fire red but under reducing conditions (in a smoky fire) will fire black. Absolute control over the colour of this paint was not achieved for a long time.

The next stage in the development of Pre-palatial pottery is the ware named, from the most plentiful and most attractive pottery at Seager's site, Vasiliki ware, which was made between 2500 and 2200 BC. The paint is the same as in the earlier stage, but it was

34

applied over the entire surface of the vase, and a mottled effect was obtained by holding burning twigs against the vase while it was still hot from the kiln. Extravagant shapes with long spouts were very popular.

The last stage of Pre-palatial pottery sees simple designs in a thick creamy white, at first against a mottled ground, later against a black ground: the beginnings of Kamares ware.

It remained for a young English archaeologist, Peter Warren, to fill out the picture which Seager had so brilliantly sketched. In 1967–8 he completely cleared a settlement at Fournou Korifi, near Myrtos, in south-east Crete; this settlement had lived out its whole existence between 2500 and 2200 BC, when it was burnt down and never rebuilt. The settlement consisted of flat-roofed bungalows, not unlike Cretan peasants' houses today. The walls were of mud-brick on rubble foundations, plastered inside and painted red or brown over the plaster.

Terracotta goddess from Fournou Korifi, c. 2300 BC. The figure is about eight inches tall.

35

Warren found the loom-weights and spindle-whorls of a textile industry, and a potter's shop with clay turntables which may have been the direct ancestors of the true potter's wheel. The pottery included the gaily mottled Vasiliki ware discovered by Seager some fifty years before.

There was a shrine, which contained a terracotta figure of a long-necked goddess wearing a bell-like skirt and holding a jug. And next to the shrine was a treasury for religious vases.

A few seal-stones were also found, which are among the earliest yet discovered in Crete. But what is perhaps more interesting, the bones of sheep, goats, pigs and cattle showed what a varied diet the inhabitants enjoyed; while the pips and skins of grapes suggest that they knew how to make wine.

This, then, was how the Pre-palatial people lived in East Crete. Another excavation by Richard Seager, which he made in 1908, shows how they died. He dug a group of tombs on the island of Mochlos which produced, amongst other things, some of the finest stone vases and the earliest gold jewellery to be found in Crete.

Gold jewellery from the tombs at Mochlos.

36

Communal tombs,
2500–2000 BC, on
the island of Mochlos,
looking towards
mainland Crete.

The vases were made between 2500 and 2000 BC, of brightly-coloured variegated stones. The method of manufacture was learned from Egypt where they had been making stone vases for centuries, but the delicate shapes and the choice of material reveal a typically Cretan originality. It was a laborious process to make one of these vases. The outside was blocked out by pounding with hard stones and finished by grinding with emery powder from the island of Naxos. The inside was hollowed out by a copper drill also fed with emery powder.

The graves at Mochlos also produced a considerable amount of jewellery; gold pins made in the shape of flowers, embossed diadems, pendants and chains; and beads of semi-precious stones. The patterns for this type of jewellery lay far to the east, in Babylonia, where superb examples were excavated in the 1920s by Sir Leonard Woolley at Ur of the Chaldees; but the Cretan goldsmiths, less skilful, used thinner gold and simpler methods.

Such was the state of affairs in Crete before the palaces were built. And from the patient work for over half a century of three archaeologists—the Greek, the American and the Englishman—we can see how a thousand years of growing prosperity made the next epoch, that of the palaces, almost inevitable.

37

5

Knossos: the Palace of Minos

The general situation of ancient Knossos had always been remembered—the town survived until the eighth century AD and even boasted a bishop—but the existence of the Palace was soon forgotten, except for vague memories of a maze called the 'labyrinth' in which Minos had kept the monstrous Minotaur.

There is, however, some rather surprising evidence that part of the Palace was uncovered by an earthquake in the first century AD. In the third century AD a literary forgery was composed which purported to be an eye-witness account of the Trojan War by a certain Dictys, who fought with the Greek contingent led by King Agamemnon of Mycenae. It had a preface, however, which is almost certainly founded on fact. In this preface it is stated that in the thirteenth year of the Emperor Nero (AD 67) a number of tombs at Knossos were opened up by an earthquake. A shepherd, on investigating the tombs, found in one of them a tin box containing pieces of bark with strange writing on them. He passed his find on to his master, who passed it on to the Governor of Crete, who passed it on to the Emperor. The Emperor sent for experts who announced that the writing was Phoenician, and translated it as the story of Dictys.

Now it is beyond coincidence that the West Magazines, or storerooms, of the Palace look very like tombs; and that in some of them Arthur Evans found lead-lined cavities (the 'tin boxes') and inscribed clay tablets ('bark, with mysterious writing'). So although the story itself is a fake, the circumstantial evidence must surely be regarded as genuine.

After this rather curious episode there is silence for some sixteen centuries until the year 1876, when an amateur archaeologist from

Heraklion, Minos Kalokairinos, conducted a small excavation on the great mound of Kefala where tradition placed the labyrinth, and found the same West Magazines which were associated with the story of Dictys. His most important discoveries were twelve large storage jars, one of which he presented to the British Museum. Most of his collection was, regrettably, destroyed in the Cretan insurrection of 1897.

He did not pursue his investigations further, but word of his efforts reached the great Heinrich Schliemann, who had recently excavated at Troy and Mycenae as well as other prehistoric sites in Greece. He accordingly came to Crete in 1886 and started negotiations to buy the site from its Turkish owners. For three years he bargained without success, and finally gave up the struggle in 1889, having achieved nothing but a small trial excavation which he had been allowed to make.

In 1894 Arthur Evans arrived in Crete—the man who was to have such a spectacular impact on Cretan archaeology. He was born in 1851, the son of Sir John Evans, a rich man and himself a noted archaeologist. He became by profession a press correspondent in the Balkans, where he often got into trouble, and was once imprisoned for his Liberal views and his sympathy with those peoples who were trying to shake off the Turkish yoke. But he was also a keen amateur archaeologist, and in 1884 had been made Keeper of the Ashmolean Museum in Oxford. He continued to pay visits to the Balkans and to Greece, sometimes as the Liberal sympathiser, sometimes as the student of antiquity.

Seal and impression of two acrobats, Knossos.

It was meeting Schliemann which quickened his interest in Mycenaean civilisation; and it was Mycenaean seal-stones which led him to Crete in 1894. Six years later, Evans at last succeeded in buying the site of Knossos and obtaining from the Cretan authorities a permit to excavate, with the exceptional privilege of retaining some of his finds; and in 1900 he started to dig.

D. G. Hogarth, Director of the British School at Athens, who accompanied him at the start of the excavations, wrote: 'For us then and no others . . . Minos was waiting when we rode out from Candia (Heraklion). Over the very site of his buried throne a desolate donkey drooped, the only living thing in view. He was driven off, and the digging of Knossos began.'

Evans's half-sister Joan Evans later wrote in the same spirit: 'He had come to the site in hope of finding a seal impression and a clay tablet, and Time and Chance had led him to discover a civilisation.'

39

Evans engaged thirty workmen, both Moslems and Christians, to set an example of international harmony, and got down to work. They were lucky from the start. On the second day they found the remains of an ancient house, with pottery and fragments of frescoes. Evans noted the resemblance of the pottery to that from the Kamares Cave. On the fourth day they uncovered a wall of what Evans recognised as the Palace, and he noted that it had been destroyed by fire. On the seventh day he found what he had come for: 'A kind of baked clay bar, rather like a stone chisel in shape, though broken at one end, with script on it and what appear to be numerals.'

He increased his labour force to a hundred and found more frescoes, more walls, a hoard of inscribed tablets. He wrote to his father:

'The great discovery is whole deposits, entire or fragmentary, of clay tablets analogous to the Babylonian but with inscriptions in the prehistoric script of Crete. I must have about seven hundred pieces by now. It is extremely satisfactory, as it is what I came to Crete seven years ago to find, and it is the coping to what I have already put together. These inscriptions engraved on the wet clay are evidently the work of practised scribes, and there are also many figures no doubt representing numerals. A certain number of characters are pictographic, showing what the subject of the documents was.'

Seal and impression of a priest holding a sacred bird, Knossos.

He was right as far as he went; but he never succeeded in deciphering this script, which he was soon to call Linear B, and it was left for Michael Ventris to make the decisive break-through in 1953.

Evans had now found what he had come to Crete to seek—ample evidence of the prehistoric script he felt sure he had glimpsed on the engraved seal-stones in the antique dealer's shop in Athens. But he had found much more: in the ruins of the Palace of Knossos he had found a whole lost civilisation. With a touching lack of false modesty he wrote to his father in 1900: 'The Palace of Knossos was my idea and my work, and it turns out to be such a find as one could not hope for in a lifetime or in many lifetimes.'

So Evans, at the age of fifty, was to devote the rest of his own lifetime and his considerable personal fortune to the excavation and restoration of Knossos. He dug there for over twenty-five years, loyally assisted by Duncan Mackenzie, Piet de Jong, John Pendlebury, 'Squire' Hutchinson, and others. He published a monumental work, *The Palace of Minos*, which has become the Bible of scholars

40

The Palace at Knossos.

1 West Porch
2 Corridor of the Procession
3 Palace Shrine
4 Stepped porch
5 Throne Room
6 Grand Staircase

7 Hall of the Double Axes
8 'Queen's Megaron'
9 Pillar Hall
10 Store-rooms
11 Royal Road, to Little Palace

41

in this field. Right up to his death in 1941, at the age of ninety, Knossos absorbed all his time and attention.

Within the first five years of the excavation he had laid bare most of the Palace, and restored it to the state in which thousands of visitors every year see it now. He has been criticised for over-restoring, and it is certainly true that the most eye-catching parts of the Palace are almost completely modern. But Evans's successor, John Pendlebury, made a spirited defence of this method of restoration:

'With a building such as this, rising many storeys in height, it has always been a question of how to preserve the evidence of upper floors. This has been solved by roofing in various parts of the Palace and by raising to their proper level the door-jambs, column-bases and paving-blocks which had fallen into the rooms below.

'Without restoration, the Palace would be a meaningless heap of ruins . . .'

The Palace had three entrances, on the west, north, and south, all of them remarkably unobtrusive considering the magnificence of the building. Today the entrance is from the west, across a large open court fronted by the imposing West Façade, still bearing the marks of the great fire which destroyed the Palace around 1400 BC.

Round the corner from this western entrance, in the first spring of the excavation (April, 1900), Evans found the shattered pieces of a fresco amongst a rubble of fallen masonry. When the remains of the fresco were pieced together, they showed the first picture of what the Minoans had looked like. Two figures had survived, but they had originally formed part of a much larger mural which had gone all the way round the South Propyleum, depicting a whole procession of young men carrying tall funnel-shaped vessels. Evans described this spectacular find in his diary:

'The figure is life size, the flesh colour of a deep reddish hue like that of figures on Etruscan tombs and the *Keftiu* of Egyptian paintings. The profile of the face is a noble type; full lips, the lower showing a slight peculiarity of curve below. The eye is dark and slightly almond shaped . . . The arms are beautifully modelled . . . The waist is of the smallest . . . It is far and away the most remarkable human figure of the Mycenaean age that has yet come to light.'

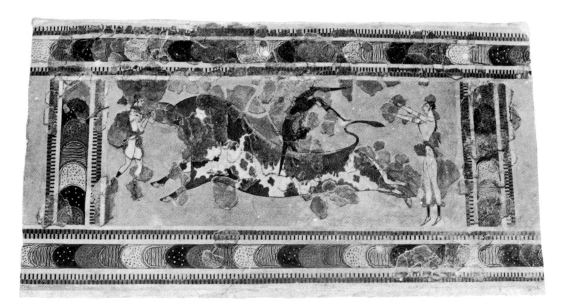

Fresco at Knossos showing the bull-sports.

From the Propyleum the way into the heart of the Palace leads through what were once royal audience rooms, through what Evans called 'a crescendo of spacious corridors, peristyles and halls, served beyond by a stately staircase ... to the *piano nobile*, or principal floor.'

The focal point of the palace was the Central Court, which measured 160 feet by 90 feet. It was here, in all probability, that the celebrated Minoan bull-sports were held. One of the frescoes Evans found vividly depicted this extraordinary spectacle:

> 'The girl acrobat in front seizes the horns of a coursing bull at full gallop, one of which seems to run under her left armpit. The object of her grip clearly seems to be to gain a purchase for a backward somersault over the animal's back, such as is being performed by the boy. The second female performer behind stretches out both her hands as if to catch the flying figure or at least to steady him when he comes to earth the right way up.'

As he dug, Evans was preoccupied with memories of the legends of Minos and the Minotaur that lurked in the labyrinth. Were these bull-sports not the origin of the story of the Athenian tribute of youths and maidens to be sacrificed each year? On all sides Evans was finding abundant evidence of bull-worship.

'What a part these creatures play here! On the frescoes and reliefs, the chief design of the seals, on a steatite vase, above the gate it

43

may be of the Palace itself. Was not some one or other of these creatures visible on the ruined site in the early Dorian days, which gave the actual tradition of the Bull of Minos?'

To the east of the Central Court were the Private Apartments of Minos and his queen, served by a Grand Staircase, rising at least one storey above the Central Court and descending two storeys below it, down the slope of the hill. This staircase was excavated with great skill by Evans, who preserved the upper levels and shored them up with concrete supports while excavating the lower ones:

'The Grand Staircase, as thus reconstituted, stands alone among ancient architectural remains. With its charred columns solidly restored in their pristine hues, surrounding in tiers its central walls, its balustrades rising, practically intact, one above the other, with its imposing fresco of the great Minoan shields on the back wall of its middle gallery now replaced in replica, and its still well-preserved gypsum steps ascending to four landings, it revives, as no other part of the building, the remote past.'

The lower part of the Grand Staircase.

The King's apartments downstairs had a large ante-room; a row

44

Jointed terracotta water pipes at Knossos.

of columns with folding doors enclosed the King's private audience room, and here Evans placed a replica of his throne. The Queen's apartments nearby have a vivid sense of intimacy, of light and air, the walls alive with graceful murals of dolphins; next door was the Queen's bathroom, with a terracotta bath-tub. The tub had to be filled and emptied by hand, but apart from this inconvenience the Palace had a complex and sophisticated plumbing system, to carry away rainwater from the roofs, and to serve water closets:

'The elaborate drainage system of the Palace and the connected sanitary arrangements excite the wonder of all beholders. The terracotta pipes, with their scientifically-shaped sections, nicely interlocked, which date from the earliest days of the building, are quite up to modern standards.'

What life in the Palace was like can be seen from the surviving frescoes, all of which were in a very fragmentary state. The style is the first truly naturalistic style to be found in ancient art, and is of the highest quality. The Priest-King fresco depicts a young king walking in a flower garden, wearing a tightly-belted kilt, a feathered crown, and a gold chain round his neck. The body is modelled in low relief. The painting is much restored (including the entire face), but enough of the original survives to give an idea of its brilliance.

Another wall-painting, the Camp-Stool fresco, gives a marvellously vivacious picture of the courtiers who surrounded royalty at

45

Knossos. It shows a group of young people sitting on folding stools (at a picnic, perhaps) and drinking each other's health. The young Minoan ladies are seen talking animatedly and dressed in the height of flamboyant fashion—so much so that one of them, an exquisite head and shoulders showing a girl with a tip-tilted nose and pert expression, has come to be known as 'La Parisienne':

'These scenes of feminine confidences, of tittle-tattle and society scandals, take us far away from the productions of classical art in any age. Such lively genre and rococco atmosphere bring us nearer to quite modern times.'

The Priest-King fresco.

46

The faience Snake
Goddess.

These paintings flanked a fresco which Evans believed showed a
shrine of a Minoan goddess. The principal shrine of the Palace itself
was on the west side of the Centre Court. This is where the Minoan
Snake Goddess seems to have been worshipped, for the sacred
snake was regarded as the guardian spirit of a Cretan household. In a
large cist in a room behind the shrine, Evans found two beautiful
figurines made of faience (a body of powdered quartz formed in a
mould, painted with coloured glazes, and fired: a process which
Minoan craftsmen had learned from Egypt). The figurines are
exceptionally lifelike, two women wearing low-cut dresses with
flounced skirts, and both carrying a snake in each hand. They are

47

Kamares ware

This jar is typical of
the earliest pottery of
the second palaces

OPPOSITE
'La Parisienne' from
the Camp Stool fresco
at Knossos.

interpreted as a Snake Goddess and her attendant.

Nearby, to the north, is a shrine of a different kind, and one that
aroused great excitement when Evans found it in April 1900. It is
now known as the Throne Room suite, which was installed when the
Palace was reconstructed after the disaster of 1450 BC, and it consisted of an anteroom, the Throne Room proper, and a suite of small
rooms behind. The throne itself, made of gypsum (a soft stone,
rather like alabaster, which was quarried locally), had a high back
which was partly embedded in the stucco of the wall, and it was
flanked by low benches also of gypsum. On the wall painted heraldic
griffins attended the throne on either side; but in these paintings
the essentially Minoan love of life and nature and movement had
been replaced by the grander treatment preferred by the Mycenaeans.

Facing the throne was a sunken area which Evans at first took to
be a bath, with broad steps leading down into it. This was later
identified as a lustral basin for ritual ceremonies of purification, for
it had no plumbing arrangements. The room clearly had a religious
purpose, as a private shrine for the Priest-King; and when Evans
cleared the room he found evidence that some sort of ceremony
was taking place at the moment when the final catastrophe struck.
The floor was littered with alabaster oil-jars lying about in confusion,
and a large overturned storage jar. The walls and throne were
scorched. In *The Archaeology of Crete*, John Pendlebury saw in this
disordered room the seeds, perhaps, of the legend of Theseus and
the Minotaur, with Theseus leading a band of liberators:

'The final scene takes place in the most dramatic room ever
excavated—the Throne Room. It was found in a state of complete
confusion. A great oil-jar lay overturned in one corner, ritual
vessels were in the act of being used when the disaster came. It
looks as if the King had been hurried there to undergo, too late,
some last ceremony in the hopes of saving the people. Theseus
and the Minotaur! Dare we believe that he wore the mask of the
bull?'

Few scholars would dare, or care, to believe such a literal associ-
ation with the legend now. But Knossos was excavated at a time
when scepticism about 'myths' of the past had suddenly changed to
romantic enthusiasm. Had not Schliemann by his excavations at
Troy and Mycenae proved that the Homeric 'legends' had a kernel of
truth? Evans himself felt that he, too, had justified the validity of
the legends about Crete:

48

The Marine style

'We know now that the old traditions were true. We have before us a wondrous spectacle—the resurgence, namely, of a civilisation twice as old as that of Hellas. It is true that on the old Palace site what we see are only the ruins of ruins, but the whole is still inspired with Minos's spirit of order and organisation, and the free and natural art of the great architect Daedalus.'

Apart from excavating and restoring the great palace at Knossos, Evans created a framework for the history of Cretan culture in the Neolithic period and the Bronze Age which is basically valid to this day, nearly three-quarters of a century later.

Evans discovered traces of the earliest Neolithic settlement underneath the Palace ruins by means of deep pits which he sank. He reckoned that this settlement was as early as 6000 BC, and this inspired conjecture has now been confirmed by radiocarbon dating : it is the oldest Neolithic settlement in Europe.

There were hardly any structural remains of the first palace which was built about 2000 BC and destroyed by earthquake about 1700 BC; it had probably started as a set of separate buildings, grouped around a central court, which were gradually connected together to look much like the second palace that replaced it. But Evans found sufficient pottery remains of the First-palatial period to give a clear picture of the changing styles of palace life.

Evans saw at once that it was like the pottery which had caused so much surprise when it was found in the Kamares Cave in the 1890s. Unlike earlier Cretan pottery it was thrown on the wheel, and the shapes in consequence are more delicate, and frequently imitate metal originals. The decoration is an elaboration of the white-on-black style of the latest Pre-palatial pottery; the patterns are drawn in white, red, orange and yellow against a black ground. In the finest examples they throb and revolve, rather like the patterns on a Paisley shawl. This is one of the most satisfying pottery styles ever to have been invented, and it stands comparison with the finest Chinese porcelain.

The Palace style

The pottery found in the second palace built after the earthquake destruction of 1700 BC starts as a development of the Kamares style, but not a very successful development. The colour scheme is the same—but the vivacity of Kamares is replaced by a more monumental treatment. A large jar with palm-trees, typical of the new movement, exhibits a stateliness verging on the pompous.

The State Apartments at Knossos as they appear today.

About 1600 BC experiments were being made with dark-on-light

49

decoration, and by 1550 an entirely new style had evolved in this manner. Between 1550 and 1500 BC the favoured patterns were spirals, and life-like studies of plants; between 1500 and 1450 the repertoire is enriched by the Marine style, one of the finest of all Minoan pottery styles. The entire surface of the vase is filled with a riot of sea-creatures—octopus, argonauts, fish, or dolphins, against a background of rocks, sponges, and seaweed.

This was the last purely Minoan style to develop before the catastrophe of 1450 BC laid waste the eastern half of Crete and damaged Knossos itself. The last pottery style in use at the Palace of Knossos, named by Evans the Palace style, was introduced by the Mycenaean conquerors who now moved in and repaired and slightly altered the stricken palace. In this new style earlier motifs are stiffened into a rigid pose and spontaneity is replaced by grandeur, as in the griffins in the Throne Room frescoes. This Palace style had only just started to reach other Cretan centres when Knossos itself was destroyed by fire around 1400 BC, never to be inhabited as a palace again.

The same change in style took place in the seal-engraver's art.

Arthur Evans in the Throne Room shortly after its excavation.

50

About 1900 BC the engravers had first turned their hands to harder stones like rock-crystal, cornelian, agate, amethyst and jasper. Their favourite subjects were geometrical patterns, hieroglyphic signs, and studies of animals. The second palace saw the climax of this art at Knossos. The subjects, religious scenes and studies of people and animals, are rendered with an astonishing truth to Nature. Between 1450 and 1400, however, during the Mycenaean occupation, the craftsmen favoured a more monumental style, and groups of animals, real or imaginary, in heraldic poses, were common subjects.

At the time of its final destruction, the Palace of Knossos was almost a small city in itself. There were extensive workshops, and at basement level a number of store-rooms in which the Palace treasures and the provisions for the occupants were stored. There were enormous clay jars for oil and grain, some of them as tall as a man. There were quarters for the officials who ran the Palace administration and kept the archives; and it was in these archives that Evans found the hundreds of clay tablets which had been baked hard by the last conflagration.

The restored Throne Room today.

There was a natural, spontaneous quality in the way in which the Palace had spread to meet the needs of the moment. The Minoans,

51

The Royal Road. Evans called this 'the oldest road in Europe'.

secure in their naval power, had seen no need for fortifications, so there was plenty of room to expand whenever necessary.

Evans found many official buildings all round the Palace, which he took to be the houses of the Palace staff. To the north-west is a stepped area looking like a squared-off theatre. From it a road—the Royal Road as Evans called it—leads to the Little Palace some 250 yards away. Although much smaller than the Palace, it was every bit as grand and may well have been a second residence for the King himself. In it was found a magnificent ritual vessel of steatite (a very soft stone also known as soapstone) in the form of a bull's head. The horns were of gilded wood, the eyes of rock-crystal very realistically painted, and the muzzle was of shell. The total effect is amazingly lifelike.

This Little Palace was built about 1600 BC, and was probably inhabited by royalty as their principal dwelling after the main Palace was destroyed about 1400 BC. It was finally deserted about 1200 BC, at the same time as the squatters who had taken over parts of the ruined Palace abandoned Knossos for ever.

Sir Arthur Evans left a great legacy to Cretan archaeology. In 1906 he had built the Villa Ariadne as his home and his operational base. In 1928 he generously gave the Palace site to the British School at Athens. After the war it was given to the Greek nation, but as far as excavation is concerned, Knossos remains a British preserve.

The most recent task undertaken by the British School is the excavation of a building adjoining the Little Palace; Evans called it the Unexplored Mansion, for he had deliberately left it unexcavated so that future archaeologists could apply their skills to it. The site was much disturbed, as it had been robbed in places for building stone as far down as the foundations, but the remains of a magnificent façade of squared limestone blocks suggest that in its day it had been quite as grand as the Little Palace. It is too soon to be certain of its history, but it looks as if it was built about 1450 BC, suffered a major catastrophe about 1400 BC, and was finally deserted about 1200 BC.

One last reminder of the end of Knossos has been uncovered in recent years. In 1923 Evans had attempted to excavate a site at Archanes, a few miles south of Knossos, where he had found Minoan ruins, but the area was so built over that he was forced to abandon his investigations. However, in 1964, a young Greek archaeologist called John Sakellarakis explored the area; he succeeded in buying up and demolishing a number of modern houses,

Gold necklace from the royal tomb at Archanes

53

and underneath them he exposed part of a palace belonging to the fifteenth century BC.

It is highly unlikely that there would have been an independent royal establishment so close to Knossos itself; it must surely have been a satellite palace for other members of the Knossos dynasty. The following year, in 1965, Sakellarakis excavated another site here which seemed to confirm this theory: it was a beehive tomb of the Mycenaean type in a hillside overlooking the Archanes palace. The principal chamber had been robbed long ago, but a side chamber was found completely intact. In it was a clay chest-shaped coffin containing the bones of a woman, remains of her clothing, and much high-quality gold jewellery. There were more than 140 pieces in all: beads, ornaments sewn on clothing, and five signet rings. This lady had died about 1400 BC, at the end of the brief period of Mycenaean control. If she was a princess of Knossos, as seems highly likely, she may well have been the last.

Arthur Evans's excavation of the Little Palace.

54

6

Phaestos and Ayia Triada

Crete had always interested the Italians, partly because of all the Greek islands it is most like Italy, partly because it was for so long under Venetian rule. So for the Italian archaeologist, Federico Halbherr, who came from the neighbourhood of Venice, Crete had a double fascination.

He had been prospecting there during the last years of the Turkish occupation, and when Crete gained its freedom in 1898 he was one of the first to claim the right to excavate under the new regime. The Italians were allotted the Mesara Plain in the south, where they had already started to explore the classical city of Gortyn, and were soon to excavate the two Minoan sites of Phaestos and Ayia Triada.

The general position of the ancient city of Phaestos had been identified by Captain Spratt in the 1850s, but conditions were not suitable for excavation. In 1894, however, Halbherr saw some prehistoric objects which had come to light in a tomb near the classical city of Phaestos, and he decided to look for the adjoining settlement. He soon found ruined buildings and pieces of prehistoric pottery, but was prevented from excavating by the political situation. In 1900 things were very different and he was able to begin excavating at the same time that Arthur Evans was starting his work at Knossos.

The bulk of the Palace was laid bare in three years, but—although the excavators did not know it then—there was a great deal more to do. In fact work has been going on there, on and off, ever since and there is still more to find.

Like Evans at Knossos, the Italians have been doing restoration

55

The north-east wing of the Palace today.

work on the site; but their methods are much less drastic than his. In fact they have done little more than preserve and consolidate the excavated ruins, and although there is something to be said on Evans's side, most people prefer what they see at Phaestos.

Of the four Minoan palaces which have been discovered in Crete, the Palace of Phaestos gives the best idea of what the First-palatial buildings were like, because in some places the second palace was set some way back from the ruins of the earlier one. Unfortunately all the south side and over half the east side have fallen down the hill and are lost for ever.

As at Knossos, the first palace was built about 2000 BC. When it was destroyed by the earthquake about 1700 BC a new one was built over the ruins. This second palace was burnt down about 1450 BC and abandoned. As far as we can tell, it was never rebuilt or re-occupied as a palace, although parts of it seem to have been put in order and used for religious purposes much later, in about 1200 BC.

The ancient town outside the Palace was soon rebuilt after the disaster of 1450 BC, and had a long and continuous existence. Much

56

of it still remains to be excavated, but a cemetery with burials from about 1400 to 1100 BC shows that there were still people of importance living in Phaestos.

We know that this place was already by Minoan times called Phaestos, its name in classical times, because the name is mentioned in inscriptions found at Knossos.

The Palace is very reminiscent of Knossos, and it seems that the architect was copying Knossos in its general outlines. There are,

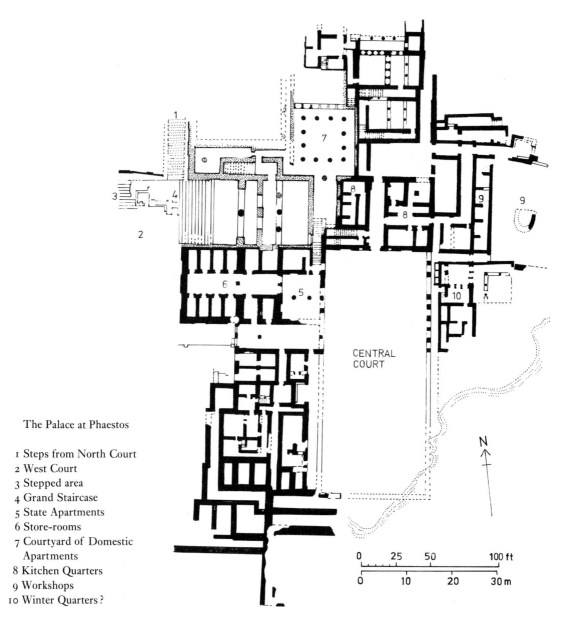

The Palace at Phaestos

1 Steps from North Court
2 West Court
3 Stepped area
4 Grand Staircase
5 State Apartments
6 Store-rooms
7 Courtyard of Domestic
  Apartments
8 Kitchen Quarters
9 Workshops
10 Winter Quarters?

57

however, two main differences. The setting at Phaestos is far more beautiful than that of Knossos, for Phaestos was built on a steep hilltop looking north, towards Mount Ida, and its plan was more regular and symmetrical than that of Knossos.

The approach from the North Court gave then, and gives now, a dramatic bird's-eye view of the Palace. A flight of steps leads down to the West Court. On the right a wide stepped area was probably intended for ceremonial parades and the like, while an imposing flight of steps led to what were originally the State Apartments on the first floor, but these have not survived.

From the State Apartments a stairway ran down to the Central Court, which was the same size as the one at Knossos, and like Knossos was probably the arena for the bull-sports. It was paved with flagstones, and along both the long sides were colonnades, with galleries above from which the King and the royal household could watch the spectacle.

On the west side of the Central Court beyond the State Apartments were the Palace store-rooms, with enormous pottery jars for oil and grain. South of the State Apartments the Italian archaeologists discovered suites of rooms, some with private bathrooms, which they believed to be the guest-rooms for important visitors.

The principal Domestic Apartments lay to the north-west, where they were grouped round a colonnaded courtyard like a medieval cloister. Facing north and looking towards Mount Ida with its snow-capped summit they would give a pleasant relief from the intense heat of summer.

The buildings immediately north of the Central Court are well preserved. There is an imposing entrance, flanked by half-columns, leading to the Kitchen Quarters on the ground floor; there was a Banqueting Hall above, and probably another storey above that. To the east of this block were the Palace workshops, which included a furnace for the smelting of copper.

The finds from Phaestos are on the whole disappointing. The first palace, however, produced quantities of gaily-coloured vases in the Kamares style, some as thin as eggshell, others flamboyantly decorated with large attached pottery models of flowers and the like. The early potters of Phaestos were every bit as skilful as their colleagues at Knossos, even if their taste was not so sure.

The pottery from the second palace is also of very high quality. It is mostly decorated, as at Knossos, with patterns of spirals, flowers and grasses, and superb studies of marine life. The patterns

Brightly coloured chalice decorated with terracotta flowers—a typical example of the Kamares style at Phaestos.

58

The Phaestos Disc.
The characters have
never been deciphered.

are all in a shiny black, helped out with touches of red and white, against the yellow body of the pottery. Both the first and the second palaces produced enormous pottery storage jars.

Much the most interesting find is the so-called Phaestos Disc, which was excavated with other objects dating from about 1600 BC. It is a disc of fired clay, an inch thick by six inches in diameter, impressed on both sides with picture-writing. The signs include a man's head wearing a feather headdress, a running man, a ship, an eagle, a vase, and a house. They were impressed on the wet clay on both sides of the Disc with wooden stamps, like an early form of printing, running in a spiral from the rim towards the centre. This is not the Cretan hieroglyphic writing, nor anything like it, and no one has yet succeeded in deciphering whatever message it may contain. It is unique, and a complete mystery.

In the summer of 1902 the excavators of Phaestos, having (as they thought) completely cleared the Palace, turned their attention to another site some two miles to the north-west, where Minoan remains were visible on the surface. This new site, whose ancient name is not known, is called Ayia Triada (Holy Trinity) from a nearby Venetian church of that dedication. The first excavation

59

continued till 1905, a second from 1910 to 1914. The official publication of this excavation has not yet appeared, but a fair amount of information is available.

The site is incredibly beautiful and very fertile. From it one sees Mount Ida to the north, and the sea-shore with the West Cretan mountains behind it to the west. It lies now some way from the sea, but three thousand years ago, before the river-mouth was silted up, the sea probably came up to the foot of the hill on which it stands.

Up to 1550 BC there had been no more than a few houses on the site. But about that date a magnificent villa was built, and connected by a paved road with the Palace at Phaestos. At the same time a village was created to serve it, adjoining it on the north. The relationship between Palace and Villa is not clear, but the Villa is generally regarded as a summer residence for the King of Phaestos. That it belonged to the King is clear from the important character of the architecture, the rich interior decoration, and the high quality of the objects found in it.

Its life was short, for, like the Palace, it too was destroyed, together with the village, in the catastrophe which occurred about 1450 BC. There was evidence everywhere of burning. What happened after that is not absolutely clear, but it seems that the village was rebuilt on a grander scale almost immediately; but the Villa itself was never reoccupied by royalty. About 1200 BC, a Mycenaean hall or megaron was built over parts of the ruins; it probably served some religious purpose in connection with an open-air sanctuary, for a great number of offerings were found there, including numbers of bronze and terracotta animals, especially bulls.

The Villa has roughly the shape of a letter L, rather like half a palace. The downward stroke of the L forms the North Wing, with the Domestic and State Apartments; the horizontal stroke forms the West Wing, with servants' quarters, store-rooms and workshops.

The principal Domestic Apartments were at the junction of the two arms of the L. A long reception hall which could be subdivided by partitions opened on to a terrace with a superb view. A small courtyard led the way to a luxurious drawing-room with a floor and walls of gypsum, and gypsum benches round the walls. Leading off it was a bedroom.

In the same general area the excavators found an Archive Room in which were clay tablets inscribed with the writing known as Linear A; this was the earlier form of Cretan Linear script, and has not yet been deciphered. The Archive Room also contained a number

Jug with leaf decoration from the second palace at Phaestos

60

1 Reception Hall
2 Courtyard
3 Drawing-room
4 Archive Room
5 Room with frescoes
6 Store-room for ingots
7 State Apartments
8 Sanctuary
9 Steps to North Ramp
10 Shops
A B C D Megaron
▬▬▬ = before 1450 BC
════ = after 1450 BC

VILLAGE

NORTH WING

North Ramp

N

WEST WING

0 25 50 100 ft

0 10 20 30 40 50m

The Villa and village at Ayia Triada

of lumps of clay marked with impressions from seal-stones and signet rings showing scenes of animals.

Rather to their surprise, in what was clearly a service area, the excavators found, next to the Archive Room, a very small room elaborately decorated with fine frescoes; among them were scenes of a lady seated in a garden and a cat stalking a pheasant. Nearby was a store-room containing nineteen enormous ingots of copper, each weighing about 500 lbs. These ingots were imported from Cyprus, where the copper was mined, for the manufacture of bronze, a process which consisted of alloying the copper with tin. They were specially shaped so that they could be carried by two men, and were exported all over the Mediterranean. Other store-rooms in this part of the Villa contained enormous pottery jars for oil and grain.

Then come the State Apartments, which must originally have

61

A young king (*right*) greets an official outside his palace on this relief vase of serpentine.

been very imposing, with gypsum floors and walls panelled with alabaster. A fine staircase led up to the vanished reception rooms on the first floor.

A number of precious objects were found in the ruins of the Villa; they had been buried in 1450 BC at the time of the destruction and never recovered. Among them are three superb stone vases of serpentine which had fallen from an upper floor. On them are carved scenes in low relief, which reveal more about life in Crete in the fifteenth century BC than any other objects found so far. They were originally plated with gold leaf in imitation of embossed vases of pure gold like the two superb Vapheio cups found near Sparta. The artistic quality and lifelike appearance of these carvings are truly amazing.

62

The surviving half of a serpentine vase showing a seed-sowing festival.

One shows a young king standing outside his palace. He wears a kilt, a tight belt, high boots, and a jewelled collar, and holds a staff of office in his right hand. He is receiving an official dressed much like himself but also carrying on his right shoulder a long sword, and on his left shoulder a ceremonial sprinkler. He is attended by three men carrying the skins of sacrificed bulls, which will probably be made into those enormous shields of figure of eight form which are so often represented in Minoan art.

Another vase has lost its bottom half, but the carving on the top half makes the subject clear enough. It is a procession of people in a seed-sowing festival. Most of them carry on their shoulders hoes with willow-shoots attached to the ends. Their leader wears a cloak made like a pine cone, and there are also four singers and a dancer.

The third vase, which is rather badly damaged, shows scenes of boxing matches and bull-jumping sports.

The village to the north of the Villa was also destroyed about 1450 BC, but, unlike the Villa, it was immediately rebuilt. The chief point of interest is a colonnade running down the east side, behind which is a row of eight shops, the first Minoan shops to have been found so far. Money had not yet been invented, nor would be for another seven hundred years, so the Cretans must have had some form of barter.

63

The excavators also found a number of tombs near the Villa. In one was a magnificent sarcophagus dating from between 1450 and 1400 BC. It is made of limestone and decorated with frescoes of religious subjects. Each end shows two goddesses in a chariot, one drawn by goats, the other by griffins. On one of the long sides a pipe-player and three women approach a table; on it is a trussed bull and below it two calves crouch. In front, a priestess makes an offering at an altar. Beyond the altar stands a double axe on a shelf, a bird perching on it, and behind it is a shrine. The other side contains two scenes. On the left a woman pours liquid into a jar set between two double axes. Behind her stand a woman carrying two more jars and a man in a long gown playing a lyre. On the right, a dead man stands in front of his tomb. Three men carry gifts to him: two figures of animals and a model boat. The lifelike quality of the painting is truly remarkable at such an early date; but as a religious document, it poses more questions than it answers.

In 1959 the Italians, who are still excavating in this neighbourhood, discovered an important early circular tomb for multiple burials at Kamilari, near Ayia Triada. It is unusually large for this type of tomb, measuring twenty-four feet across the inside, with walls nearly five feet thick, and had probably been completely vaulted in stone, which is also very unusual. The dead were buried in it for at least four hundred years, from 2000 BC, when it was built, until about 1600 BC.

Most of the things buried here with the dead are of the usual kind—stone vases, pottery, seal-stones and articles of bronze—but three terracotta groups, of about 1600 BC, are of exceptional interest for the information they give us about Minoan religion.

The first shows a shrine, or perhaps a tomb. Two people are bringing offerings to two seated couples, who will be gods if it is a shrine, or the ghosts of the dead if it is a tomb. In the second group, four men are dancing in a circle with arms linked. Such dances can be seen in Greece to this day, and it is astonishing they have survived almost unchanged for nearly four thousand years. The third group consists of two women squatting on the ground, kneading cakes at a table, while a third person looks out through a door at a sanctuary. Are the women preparing a funeral feast, or perhaps an offering for the dead man's tomb?

However much these groups may puzzle us, it is probably safe to say that they are all connected in some way with funeral customs.

OPPOSITE A ritual vessel in the shape of a bull's head from the Little Palace at Knossos.

64

7

Mallia

In the 1850s Captain Spratt noticed some ancient ruins at a spot near the village of Mallia, some twenty-five miles east of Heraklion, on the north coast of Crete. He wrote:

'The site is upon a rugged piece of rising ground on the east side of a torrent-bed with a small cove at its mouth, where small boats could be sheltered when hauled ashore. The remains consist chiefly of some few foundations of ancient habitations, portions of cyclopean terraces or walls, and a massive platform about ninety-five feet square, formed of large slabs of limestone, which must have supported or been the approach to a temple. This latter, until a few years since, lay buried three or four feet beneath a reddish soil that had accumulated over it, when, a shepherd accidentally discovering a few thin plates or scales of gold in the surface soil, the inhabitants of Malia, hoping that it indicated a mine of treasure beneath, laboured diligently for several weeks in excavating the locality, but were rewarded with a few ounces of the precious metal only, which was found in the form of scales or thin plates, that seemed to have covered some statue of baser material. Perhaps it was a statue to the goddess Britomartis (who, as shown by several authors, was anciently worshipped in this neighbourhood), and probably stood upon the platform without a covered building to enclose it.'

The unofficial excavation described by Captain Spratt was brought to a sudden close when a man engaged in it was killed by a fall of earth, and nothing was then done until 1915, when the Cretan archaeologist Joseph Hazzidakis undertook a scientific investigation.

The Palace at Phaestos.

65

The Central Court at Mallia today.

In two campaigns, in 1915 and 1919, he uncovered parts of an important building which he at once recognised as a palace; and he also found portions of the ancient town, and of a cemetery by the sea.

The year 1921 saw a joint Cretan-French excavation, and in the following year the rights to excavate the site were transferred to the French School at Athens. By 1932 the Palace had been cleared and many tombs dug, and the excavators transferred their attention to the outlying houses, with which they are still occupied.

The ancient name of this site is not known, but it is very likely that it was Milatos, the mother-city of Miletus in Asia Minor. The first palace there was built in about 2000 BC and badly damaged in about 1700 BC by an earthquake. The second palace, which took its place, was soon erected on the same site, incorporating much of its predecessor, and stood till it was destroyed by fire in about 1450 BC. Although the outlying houses were rebuilt and occupied for a few more centuries, the Palace itself was never reoccupied. In consequence, in spite of repeated looting by treasure-seekers, the ground plan is still more or less intact.

Mallia was smaller and less elegant than Knossos, but in its overall plan it was much the same, apart from a few individual peculiarities. It is approached from the west, where, as at Knossos, there was an

66

imposing West Façade of squared masonry, but no monumental entrance. There were three entries, on the north, south and east.

The Central Court had an altar in its centre and was bordered on the north by a row of columns and on the east by a row of columns alternating with square piers, each connected to each other by grilles. It was partly these grilles which led the scholar Walter Graham to the view that the famous bull-sports took place in the Central Courts of the palaces, for the grilles would certainly have protected the spectators from being trampled by the bulls.

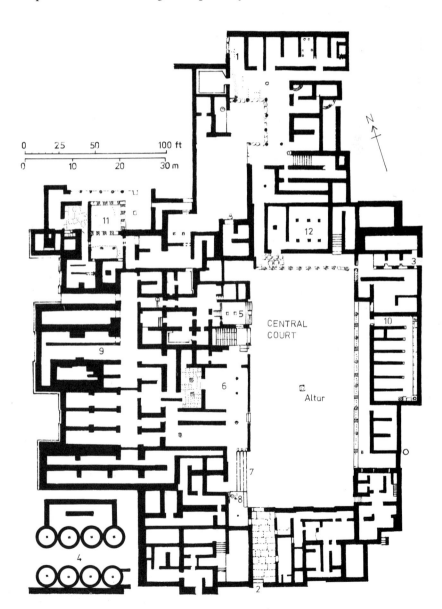

The Palace at Mallia

1 North entrance
2 South entrance
3 East entrance
4 Cisterns or granaries
5, 6 Religious rooms
7 Grand Staircase
8 Kernos
9 Store-rooms
10 Store-rooms
11 Domestic Apartments
12 Kitchen

67

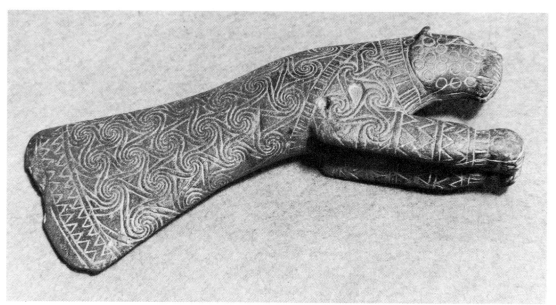

Stone axe-head in the shape of a panther.

On the west side of the Court were rooms used for religious purposes, in one of which were found two treasures: a long bronze sword with a gilt blade and an amethyst and crystal hilt, and a sacred axe-head carved in the shape of a panther.

South of these rooms a monumental staircase led to the State Apartments on the upper floor. On the left of the staircase was set a 'kernos', a large disc-shaped stone with a circular depression in the centre and smaller depressions round the rim. Its purpose is unknown but it may well have been, as in the later worship of the Greek goddess Demeter, for offerings of fruits and seeds. We know that in classical times Demeter was a popular goddess in Crete, and a sanctuary in her honour has recently been excavated at Knossos.

Further west, at ground level, were store-rooms. The east side of the Court was also devoted to store-rooms—for oil—and not (as at Knossos) to domestic apartments. The Domestic Apartments were situated, as at Phaestos, in the north-west section, looking out on to a garden. Hereabouts, under the floors of the second palace and in the debris of the first, were found two ceremonial swords, one with a figure of an acrobat embossed in gold on the pommel. East of the Domestic Apartments were the workshops of an ivory-worker and a coppersmith.

To the north of the Court was a large hall with six pillars which had supported an upper floor. By comparison with Phaestos and Zakro, this may well have been the Kitchen Quarters, and the Banqueting Hall would have been above.

68

The area to the south of the Central Court contained a small sanctuary but was probably devoted chiefly, as at Knossos, to stores and workshops.

Outside the Palace there was a flourishing town which is still in the process of excavation. In the town were discovered the remains of a gem-engraver's workshop of about 1900 BC, with tools (files, borers and polishers) and a number of unfinished seals, some of which had been spoiled and thrown out.

To the north of the Palace was a large cemetery. It was much robbed during the Turkish occupation, but one stone tomb in particular produced some important finds. It was a rectangular building with many rooms, erected about 2000 BC and continuing in use for royal burials as a sort of House of the Dead until about 1600 BC. Its modern name of Chrysolakkos (the Gold Hole) is due to the fact that it proved a source of gold to the local tomb-robbers, who were particularly active and successful in the 1880s.

The most important object to be excavated here by the French is a gold pendant of about 1700 BC in the shape of two hornets heraldically posed on either side of a honeycomb. From it hang three discs. The Cretan goldsmith, learning perhaps from a Syrian master, has combined with telling effect the advanced Western Asiatic processes of embossing, filigree and granulation and the result is a masterpiece by any standards.

There is in the British Museum a treasure of stone beads, gold

The 'kernos' at Mallia may have been an offering table for first-fruits.

69

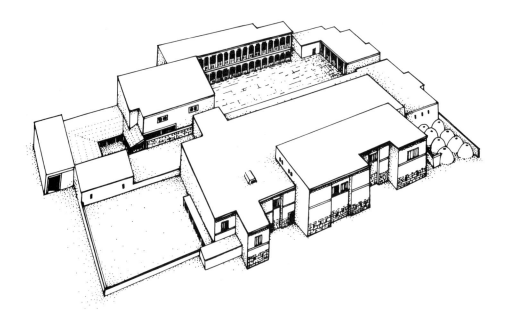

Conjectural restoration
of the Palace at Mallia

ornaments and a gold cup, which is known as the Aegina Treasure, because when the Museum bought it in 1892 the hoard was said to have been found in a tomb on that island. Tomb-robbers, however, will seldom tell the truth about where their loot comes from, and a recent examination of the Treasure has shown many similarities between it and the hornet jewel and other objects from Chrysolakkos. Since, moreover, the Treasure was bought at a time when the robbers were most active at Chrysolakkos, it has been suggested that it came from there and not from Aegina.

The two finest objects from the Aegina Treasure are a gold cup with embossed spirals, and a pendant showing a Minoan god of nature standing in a field of lilies and holding a water-bird in each hand. The pendant is hung with discs, like those of the hornet jewel. It is equally influenced by the technical processes of Western Asia and the style of Egyptian art but, like the hornet jewel, it is a truly Minoan work of art.

8

Zakro: a newly-discovered Palace

In 1852 Captain Spratt had noticed the ruins of ancient buildings on the seashore near the village of Kato Zakro in East Crete. Some thirty-five years later the Italian scholar Federico Halbherr visited the place and was impressed by these ruins which, as he rightly saw, belonged to a very early period. Indeed, had he not been preoccupied with more important matters he would have asked the owners of the land for permission to excavate. He did, however, buy for the Museum at Heraklion some ancient pottery which had been dug up on the site by the villagers some years before.

Soon after, in 1894, Arthur Evans visited the site and was equally impressed. On the strength of what he saw and what he deduced, he recommended it to D. G. Hogarth, Director of the British School at Athens, as being well worth excavating for Minoan remains, since it possessed a natural port, 'the last on the directest sea-route from the Aegean to the Cyrenaic shore'.

Accordingly in 1901 Hogarth undertook an excavation. He proved the site to be an important Minoan settlement with rich houses containing much pottery of the highest quality, bronze tools, and a deposit of clay seal-impressions:

'There was scattered over a small and roughly circular space among and about the bronzes an immense number (nearly 500) of well preserved clay nodules bearing impressions of intaglios. Most of these have two or three faces, and were evidently seals attached to documents.

'The sealings all have been hardened by fire, but whether in the baking or accidentally by the conflagration which evidently destroyed the structure in which I found them, it is impossible to

71

The site of the newly-discovered Palace at Zakro.

say. The fact that they were found over a restricted and roughly circular area suggests that they had fallen all together from a height on the collapse of some receptacle in which they had been stored. Ere they fell, the floor of the chamber had been covered to a considerable depth with burnt matter and other deposit.'

He later published a detailed study of these sealings. It seems that lumps of clay, about an inch across, were pressed over the cords which bound packages or boxes of stores or rolls of papyrus documents. The clay was then impressed, while still wet, with stone seals or gold signet rings, as a mark of ownership and a guarantee against pilfering. One might compare them to a modern customs seal, but unlike a customs seal the Minoan seal used was a real work of art.

The five hundred or so sealings from this house were made by nearly a hundred and fifty different seals, sometimes as many as three impressions being made on one lump.

The subjects engraved on the seals are much more elaborate than on those from Ayia Triada, which were of roughly the same date. Commonest are gods and goddesses, religious ceremonies, mountain-top sanctuaries, and all manner of fantastic monsters. These include winged imps, winged bird-headed or goat-headed demons, lion-headed demons, griffins and sphinxes.

The fire which destroyed this house about 1450 BC burnt all its inflammable contents—and most of them were inflammable—but at the same time it 'cooked' and so preserved the clay sealings.

In spite of showing so much promise, the excavation was not continued and the site lay fallow until well after the Second World War. Meanwhile the Greek archaeologist Nicolas Platon was becoming more and more convinced that there should be a real palace here, like Knossos, Phaestos and Mallia, for there was an excellent harbour suitable for voyages to Asia Minor, the Levant and Egypt, and in the neighbourhood were rich houses, several cemeteries, and a hill-top sanctuary. The ancient name of this important centre is not known, but a suggestion that it was Dicta (Dicte) has much to recommend it.

In 1962, with the backing of the Greek Archaeological Society and two American benefactors, Mr and Mrs Leon Pomerance, he started to excavate in an area next to where Hogarth had dug. His intuition proved correct, and almost immediately he found what Hogarth had so narrowly missed, and what he would surely have found if he had returned to the site: a palace. Its main lines were soon revealed; but excavation of the outbuildings and the neighbouring houses still continues.

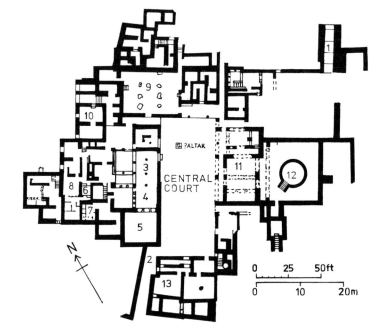

The Palace at Zakro

1 North-east entrance
2 South-west entrance
3 North reception room
4 Courtyard
5 Dining-room
6 Shrine
7 Treasury
8 Archive Room
9 Kitchen
10 Food Stores
11 Domestic Apartments
12 Courtyard with pool
13 Store-rooms

73

A number of tombs confirm the existence of a rich settlement here before the Palace was built, at least as early as 2500 BC. A palace was first built here about 2000 BC, and like the other Cretan palaces it was destroyed by an earthquake about 1700 BC. That which we see now was built over the ruins soon after 1700 BC, and lasted until it was destroyed by a terrible fire, perhaps accompanied by an earthquake, about 1450 BC. Although the houses nearby were soon repaired and inhabited, the Palace itself was never reoccupied.

The excavators started with two advantages. In the first place they had behind them sixty years of Cretan excavation: and in the second place, their site had never been reoccupied or even looted after the great destruction.

The Palace was designed on the same general lines as the other three, but with individual differences. It was somewhat smaller, but just as elaborately planned. There were two entrances, both unobtrusively sited, at the north-east and south-west respectively. The south-west entrance opened on a corridor which led to the Central Court, designed according to the usual custom as a long narrow rectangle running north and south. On the west were the State Apartments, and on the east the Domestic Apartments, both rising to two or more storeys; on the north the Kitchen Quarters; and on the south, stores and workshops.

The State Apartments were entered from the north. The first room was a reception room. Beyond it was a small courtyard to let in air and light, in which the excavators found two carved stone vases, possibly the most important of all their discoveries, which had fallen from an upper storey when the Palace was burnt down. One was a ritual vessel carved from black steatite in the form of a bull's head, very like the one which Arthur Evans had found in the Little Palace at Knossos. It, too, originally had inlaid eyes of rock crystal and horns of gilded wood. The other stone vase was an oval collared jar of a stone known as chlorite, carved in low relief with a representation of a mountain sanctuary. The entrance of the sanctuary is elaborately decorated with spirals, and on the roof four wild goats are seated heraldically, flanking a sacred stone. The rocky landscape is set with altars and sacred horns, while two more goats are shown clambering over the rocks and hawks fly overhead. The vase was originally covered with gold leaf (of which traces remain), to give it the appearance of an embossed gold vase. Such faithful representation of nature was not to be seen again in the ancient world for a thousand years. This remarkable object forms a worthy

74

This chlorite jar with a scene of a mountain sanctuary and goats was originally covered with gold leaf and is about a foot high.

A marble jar with graceful sweeping handles found near the Shrine.

companion to the three carved stone vases from Ayia Triada.

Nearby was the Dining-room, which Platon identified from the wine-jars and jugs found in it. Its walls were decorated with a pattern of running spirals worked in plaster in low relief and painted.

Behind the State Apartments was a suite of rooms used for religious purposes. There was a Shrine with a bench for idols, like those at Knossos and Gournia, and nearby a sacred bath for ritual ablutions, where a graceful marble vase with sweeping handles was found. In the same suite was a Treasury where ceremonial objects were stored in bins separated by partitions of unbaked brick. Many stone vases were found here in good condition, exquisitely carved from marble of various colours, from green porphyry quarried near Sparta, and from obsidian, a natural glass of volcanic origin which comes from Melos; and one exceptionally fine vase was carved from a block of rock crystal. The favourite shapes are elegantly tapered jars, and cups resembling communion chalices. The Treasury also contained sacred double axes of bronze, and much fine pottery.

Adjoining the Shrine on the west was an Archive Room where,

76

as at Ayia Triada, clay tablets inscribed with the Linear A script had been stored in wooden boxes.

The upper floors above the West Wing had evidently been used as store-rooms, whose contents fell into the room below at the time of the fire. Among the stores so discovered were four enormous elephant tusks, raw material for the ivory-workers; six copper ingots, like those from Ayia Triada, raw material for the bronze-workers, and plenty of bronze tools and weapons.

At the north end of the Court were the Kitchen Quarters, with a Banqueting Hall above. In the kitchen was an enormous bronze cooking-pot and a quantity of animal bones, and in an adjoining room was a complete set of bronze cooking utensils. The food stores were next to the kitchen on the west. Here fifty enormous pottery jars for storing food were found ranged along the walls, while other smaller containers held olive oil and wine. The Palace crockery was also stored in this block.

The Domestic Apartments, on the east side (as at Knossos), are not well preserved, but the general layout is clear. The only unexpected thing was a large rectangular area containing a circular pool fed by a spring and surrounded by a colonnade. Its purpose has not yet been explained, but it was probably connected with some form of religious purification.

South of the Central Court, on the ground floor, were additional store-rooms for pottery and bronze pots and pans. The Palace work-shops had been above them, and their contents fell into the rooms below when the Palace burnt down. They included unworked or partially worked stocks of ivory, stone vases, pinheads of rock crystal, pieces of faience and the craftsmen's tools.

In all, some 3,500 pottery vases were found in the Palace. The great majority were made between 1500 and 1450 BC and many are in the exquisite Marine style, which flourished especially vigorously in East Crete.

The current programme of excavation involves a number of important houses north of the Palace, some of which were partly excavated by Hogarth in 1901.

The Marine style

77

9

Gournia

In 1892 Harriet Ann Boyd (later Mrs Harriet Boyd Hawes) graduated at Smith College, Northampton, Massachusetts. For the next eight years she taught classics in the United States and also found time for frequent visits to Greece, where she worked and travelled as a student of the American School of Classical Studies in Athens.

In February 1900 she happened to be in Athens when the British, the Italians and the French were all preparing to take advantage of the liberation of Crete by starting excavations in that island. It seemed to her that her own people should have a share in this new venture. She accordingly applied to the Director of the American School, but all their funds were tied up in the excavations at Corinth and he did his best to discourage her. Nothing daunted, she appealed to D. G. Hogarth, the Director of the British School at Athens, which was next door to the American School. He gladly gave her the encouragement she needed. What was more, Arthur Evans, who was passing through Athens a week later, also met her and was equally encouraging. With their support she appealed again to her own Director and this time got permission to excavate in Crete with the funds of her Fellowship at the University of Pennsylvania.

Her first year was spent in prospecting, and in conducting a small excavation at Kavousi in East Crete, an area which had been recommended to her by Arthur Evans. The results were disappointing, for her discoveries were nearly all later than the Minoan period, but she was gaining experience.

In all her travels she was accompanied by her Greek foreman, Aristides, and by his mother, who acted as her chaperone. The journeys were all on mule-back, for there were as yet no roads.

Harriet Boyd in 1902.

The following year (1901) she returned to the neighbourhood of Kavousi to search for the Minoan settlement which she was convinced lay hereabouts, somewhere near the sea:

'At last rumor of our search reached the ear of George Perakis, peasant antiquarian of the neighbouring village of Vasiliki, and he sent word by the schoolmaster that at a place called Gournia within the deme of Kavousi but four miles west of the village he could show us a hill close to the sea, where there were broken bits of pottery and old walls.

'Accordingly on the afternoon of May 19, I met Perakis at the roadside khan near Pachyammos and proceeded westward for three quarters of a mile to a low hill densely covered with wild

OPPOSITE
Above Side panel of the painted sarcophagus from Ayia Triada, showing offerings being brought to the dead man standing outside his tomb on the right.
Below left Gold pendant, with a pair of hornets encircling a honeycomb, from a communal tomb at Mallia. *Right* Gold pendant from the Aegina Treasure showing a Minoan god of nature.

carob trees. Here we picked up a few sherds with patterns similar to those from St Anthony and peering with difficulty beneath the thick undergrowth thought we discerned the tops of ancient walls.

'In spite of many previous disappointments, we nursed a little hope, and decided to make a thorough exploration of the new site. On the following morning we were up at four o'clock preparing to leave our mountain huts. I ran up to the little church to say my prayers and kiss the hand of the Christ and coming out found the sun just touching the top of the mountains in Mirabello making them look snow-capped. Manolis left early with one mule-load, to meet workmen and take them to Gournia. We were delayed by rain. We packed and then descended—reaching the village at 8:30. It was like a page from Don Quixote. I went ahead as Royal Engineer or "sapper" with measuring rod and drawing board, Blanche followed as General. Theophane came in rear with tea-basket as Commissary Department. By noon Aristides and Manna (Aristides' mother) had come down with all the things.

'Our force of workmen was sent on the new quest, while we settled down at Kavousi in our home of the previous year, for it was mail-day and important letters had to be written. It was therefore afternoon before we could ride out to see the results of the first day's work.

'Our astonishment when we reached Gournia was indeed great. The men scattered over the hillside were in high spirits, for had not Lysimachus produced the first good find of the season—a perfect bronze spear point, and Michalis Paviadhakis, a curved bronze knife buried scarcely a foot below the surface? One man after another called us to see the potsherds, fragments of stone vases, etc. he had saved for our inspection. Perhaps the proudest workman was he who had laid bare a well-paved road, the threshold of a house and a small clay gutter. Everything pointed to a prehistoric settlement of some importance, whose existence on that site had remained unsuspected until that day. Such a discovery could not fail to appeal to the imagination of the peasants. We had no difficulty in getting new hands and began work the next morning with fifty men almost as eager as ourselves.

'Within three days we had opened houses, were following paved roads, and had in our possession enough vases and sherds bearing octopus, ivy-leaf, double axe and other unmistakably Minoan designs as well as bronze tools, seal impressions, stone vases, etc., to make it certain that we had found what we were seeking, a

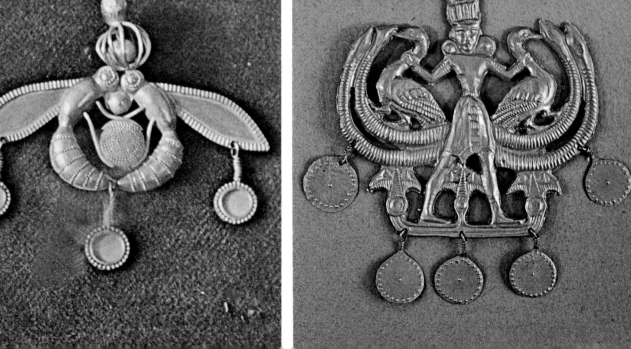

'The Young Boxers',
one of the finest
frescoes from Thera.

Bronze Age settlement of the best period of Cretan civilisation. On the night of May 22, I sent Aristides to Candia to dispatch the following telegram to the Secretary of the American Exploration Society: "Discovered Gournia Mycenaean site, street, houses, pottery, bronzes, stone jars." This was received in Philadelphia four days after the first visit paid by me, or, as far as I can learn, by any archaeologist to the hill of Gournia, although many scholars had passed within an eighth of a mile along the high road that leads from Candia to Sitia.

'We immediately petitioned the Cretan Government for special permission to excavate this new "claim" and prepared to work on a larger scale. More men were needed, trees must be cleared away, dumping grounds not likely to cover important finds must be selected, and our quarters moved nearer to the site. During the first week the evening ride home to Kavousi, along with our marching workmen, was a triumphal procession. But we could not continue to live so far from our excavations. Our new quarters at the little coast-guard station of Pachyammos were even more confined and box-like than a modern New York apartment! One room, reached by an outside staircase, did duty as a kitchen and sleeping-place for Aristides' mother; the other, narrow and lighted by one small window, accommodated Miss Wheeler and myself. To this we added the luxury of a dining-room—a bower of oleanders set up by our men on the roof of an adjoining shed— reached in undignified fashion by crawling through a kitchen window!

'By Tuesday of the second week at Gournia, our payroll numbered ninety-six men and nine girls. Considerable confusion ensued with this doubling of our force and perhaps one of the causes will seem odd and unexpected. The men came inadequately provided with names! Having been called all their lives merely Demetrios or Manolis, they were nonplussed when told this was not sufficient to distinguish them on the wage-list. Often relatives claimed the same name and I was obliged to declare severely that any man who did not provide himself with a distinctive appellation within twenty-four hours would be dismissed. I continued my policy of engaging and paying the men myself.

'Fourteen men were allowed to use the pick-axe and knife, an equal number shoveled, and the others, with the exception of a few skilled in carpentry or wall-building, carried away in baskets and barrows the earth and stones that covered the ancient town.

81

The girls washed the potsherds.

'As soon as I saw the number of small portable finds was likely to be great, I put it to the vote of our experienced diggers, the "Firsts", whether they would prefer to have a reward paid them for each object or to have their wages raised slightly and no rewards paid except a five-franc piece for every seal-stone, which, by inciting them to keep their eyes open for these small antiquities, would promote carefulness. The former method is the one in vogue with British excavators. I was glad that our men decided in favour of the second. It would have been difficult for me to have kept the additional accounts required by the reward system and to decide upon the proper amount to be given for each object. Furthermore, the second system puts the men on their honour and seems to be fairer for, after all, it is largely a matter of chance whether a man finds things or not and it is most important that he should work patiently and well wherever he is told to dig and not shirk a task which he may think will fail to bring him prizes. Much may be said, however, on the other side, especially where excavations are near towns frequented by traders or visitors. Mr Flinders Petrie tells us the reward system is absolutely necessary with fellaheen in Egypt. It has not come to my knowledge that we lost anything at Gournia through its being kept back by a workman. Severe penalties were fixed for such dishonesty. It was announced that not only would the man himself be permanently discharged, and if possible handed over to the law, but all his relatives would be dismissed also. This arbitrary decree worked well in a community composed largely of kinsmen for it ensured a strong family feeling in favour of honesty.'

In three campaigns, in 1901, 1903, and 1904, with two female companions, Harriet Boyd completely cleared a Minoan town so well preserved that it has been called a Cretan Pompeii. And in 1908 she produced the official publication of her excavation.

It is hard to know what to admire most: her courage, as a young woman, to work in what was then a male preserve in such a wild and unhealthy country; her thoroughness in completely clearing her site, a unique achievement in Cretan archaeology; or her speed in publication.

Thanks to Harriet Boyd the story of Gournia can be told in considerable detail. It was first inhabited after a fashion as early as 3000 BC, but there was no settlement of any importance till about 1650 BC when a medium-sized country town grew up there, ruled by

Gournia

83

a Governor who lived in a miniature version of the palaces. We do not know the ancient name of the place; it was not Gournia.

In common with just about every Cretan settlement, the town was burnt down about 1450 BC. Parts of it were briefly reoccupied, and it was finally deserted about 1200 BC. Consequently most of what is to be seen dates from shortly before 1450 BC.

The Governor's House was about a tenth the size of the Palace of Knossos, but was evidently modelled on it in certain essentials. It had a large open square on the south, corresponding to the Great Court of the palaces.

To the north of the Governor's House was a small shrine. It was one of the few parts of Gournia to be rebuilt after the fire of 1450 BC. In it was found a large terracotta figure of a goddess and fragments of others; all had been placed on a bench round the walls of the room, in the centre of which was a terracotta altar. The shrine was finally deserted about 1200 BC.

It was a peaceful town, with no fortifications. The roads, about five feet wide, were paved with stone. Most of them radiated out from the centre, steeply sloping and frequently stepped, but there were also a few ring roads.

More than seventy small houses were packed tightly together in a

Harriet Boyd (*second row*, *right*) with her 1904 excavation team.

84

way that reminded Miss Boyd of a modern Naples. The lower courses were of rubble, the upper of mud brick. Most were of two storeys, with flat roofs. The floors were of beaten earth or stone slabs, and the walls were plastered.

Miss Boyd gives a vivid description of the daily life of the inhabitants of this little town:

'Gournia has been called by our workmen a "biomechanike polis" —industrial town. Fishing, weaving, bronze-casting, the making of stone and terracotta vases occupied the people's time. Every tool required in a simple carpenter's chest to-day is represented, but be it understood they are all of bronze, not a scrap of iron has been found on the site. One find more than any other made the past live for me. An ancient burgher had a stone on the four sides of which were cut molds for chisel, knives and nails. This precious possession cracked and was in danger of breaking, so its prudent owner put two strips of bronze about it, wound these strips with a length of the same and perfected his bit of mending by driving in two stones as wedges. We found the stone in a doorway as if dropped by a plunderer, when he discovered its defect. From another house we obtained a bunch of the same bronze strip, wound over the fingers and tied as a neat housewife ties her linen tape to-day. In one room twenty or more clay loom-weights stood ranged above a dark line in the earth that marked a wooden shelf long burned or rotted away, and we came upon a whole kit of tools hidden in a cranny of a neighbouring wall.

'Precision, delicacy of hand and true artistic moderation appear in engraved seal-stones and in small molds for stucco decoration. The best coin-maker of Classical times could not better display the "grand style" in a small field. A painted terracotta bull's head presents in humbler material but in superior modelling the same type as the well known silver head from Mycenae.

'Gournia is especially rich in pottery, which on all prehistoric sites in the Aegean forms our chief guide for dating.'

Thus, at the very start of scientific archaeology in Crete, this brilliant American girl was able to uncover a flourishing country town which had been destroyed and forgotten three and a half thousand years ago.

10

Kythera and Thera: Minoans Overseas

Two islands outside Crete, but very much under Cretan influence, throw considerable light on Minoan civilisation—the islands of Kythera and Thera.

In 1932 Miss Sylvia Benton, an English archaeologist known principally for her excavations on the island of Ithaca, found traces of a Cretan settlement on the east side of Kythera, an island off the southernmost tip of the Greek mainland. The spot, known today as Kastri, marks the site of the city called Skandeia in classical times.

No further action was taken at that time, but in 1963 an excavation was undertaken by a joint expedition of the British School at Athens and the University of Pennsylvania Museum. In three years they uncovered much of a Bronze Age town and dug a fair number of tombs. One of the results of this excavation was to confirm Miss Benton's assertion that here was a Cretan colony, and an early one.

On the evidence of pottery from the settlement, the excavators established that there had been a Cretan colony here from as early as 2300 BC, occupied continuously for over eight hundred years. The latest occupation belongs to the period 1500–1450 BC, when there was a prosperous Cretan outpost here, possibly in contact also with Pylos and the western Peloponnese.

Like the Cretan towns, this outpost ceased to exist about 1450 BC. Unlike them, however, it was not destroyed but deserted. Perhaps the colonists chose to withdraw rather than submit when Knossos fell to the power of Mycenae. The site was not inhabited again until the sixth century AD.

Some of the best finds belong to the period 1550 to 1500 BC. They include a conical greenstone bowl, two silver cups, and some gold

Gold bead from Kythera

86

Excavating a tomb at Kythera.

beads: all imports from Crete.

The pottery of the settlement is partly Cretan, partly local imitations of Cretan; and in the last few years of its life there was also a little Mycenaean.

Another island has more to tell us. Santorini, the ancient Thera, is a volcanic island about sixty miles north of Crete. In its present state it is the submerged crater of a volcano, the remains of a catastrophic eruption which took place at some time in the past. It consists now of a number of separate islands of which the most important are the main island of Thera and a smaller one to the west of it, known as Therasia.

Geologically, working downwards from the top, it is composed of a deep layer of volcanic ash overlying a layer of pumice which rests on the soil and lava-rock of an earlier land-surface. Volcanic ash and pumice are basically the same and are known collectively as tephra. Pumice was originally the froth on top of the molten lava inside the volcano, while ash is pumice which has been ground to powder by the forces of nature.

87

Ruins of a house at Akrotiri.

In the 1860s large-scale quarrying of tephra was undertaken at Santorini to make the waterproof cement which was needed in vast quantities in Egypt for the construction of the Suez Canal. At one point on the south coast of Therasia the lower layers of the pumice were found to be studded with blocks of masonry, but the scholarly world was not made aware of this fact until, in 1866, a minor eruption of the volcano attracted a number of scientists to the island. The owner of the site and a local doctor were inspired to conduct an excavation, and they succeeded in uncovering a large house in which they found a good deal of pottery.

A French vulcanologist by the name of Fouqué took over the excavation the next year and found, amongst other things, the skeleton of an old man. He also examined similar ruins at Akrotiri in the south of Thera proper, where a ravine had been formed and the tephra had been almost completely eroded.

These discoveries led to a proper excavation at Akrotiri in 1870 by the French School at Athens. They uncovered a room with frescoes round the wall and found altogether about a hundred vases: but they had to abandon the enterprise because of the danger of a collapse. In another house which they excavated they found jars containing barley, lentils and peas. The catastrophe which buried

88

these settlements in pumice and ash had been dated by geologists to about 2000 BC. Archaeologists were not in general inclined to accept a date anything like as early as this; but, as we shall see, it was not so very far out.

After these exciting finds, apart from a small German excavation in 1899, this rich site, which promised so much more, was completely ignored. In the early 1900s, however, it became possible to classify the pottery, thanks to the British excavations on Melos and at Knossos. Most was seen to have been made locally, but some was imported from Crete, the latest being made about 1500 BC. It could then be deduced that the eruption which destroyed the settlement on Thera had taken place at that time.

Meanwhile from the 1930s onwards, the Greek archaeologist, Spiridon Marinatos, had been giving much thought to the destruction of Thera, which he sought to connect with the destruction of the Cretan settlements which happened about the same time. In 1967 he started excavating at Akrotiri, with dramatic results.

Fresco details from Thera

Marinatos has so far uncovered several large mansions built in the Cretan manner. They had a basement and two storeys above ground, and were of fine squared masonry. Interior stone staircases led to the upper storeys, whose floors were supported by central wooden columns. Many of the walls were decorated with frescoes like those of the Cretan palaces, but—in some cases—with a strong local flavour. The subjects include landscapes with flowers, birds or monkeys, antelopes, and a pair of youthful boxers.

A room excavated in 1970 is particularly instructive. It had been used for a religious ceremony. Round three of the walls was a continuous fresco of a landscape of Thera as it was before the eruption, in spring or summer. In the background are red, yellow, and green rocks with dark veins; lilies abound, with yellow stems and red flowers; and swallows fly about, singly or in pairs.

As in the previous excavations of a century ago, there was an abundance of fine pottery, some of it Cretan imports in the style of 1550 to 1500 BC. Most of it, however, was made locally and decorated in a style of local origin but strongly influenced by Cretan pottery. Characteristic of the local pottery decorations are elegant studies of flying swallows and playing dolphins.

Other articles found include lamps, bronze cooking-pots, mortars, millstones, food, stone vases, weights and tools. No valuables of gold or silver, nor any skeletons, have as yet been found here, a fact which may indicate that the inhabitants got sufficient warning to leave the island with their treasures. It is clear that there was an earthquake before the eruption, severe enough to cause considerable structural damage and force the inhabitants to evacuate the city.

After the evacuation, parts of the city were temporarily reoccupied by squatters. Over two hundred vases, some with food in them, belonged to these newcomers, who also left some bronze tools and a wooden bed and stool. The bed and the stool had rotted away, but the excavators preserved their shape by a method perfected at Pompeii; plaster was poured into the cavities left in the pumice by the rotting wood, and when it had dried, the pumice was removed from round it, leaving a perfect plaster cast.

The evidence of these excavations, and of other recent research, leads to the following tentative conclusions.

Thera was originally a fair-sized circular island dominated by a tall volcanic cone which had been dormant for many thousands of years. Nothing as yet is known of its early history before the prosperous community whose remains are now being uncovered at Akrotiri. These people were not, it would seem, Cretans but native Therans heavily influenced by the Minoan way of life. Whether at this time Thera was a Cretan colony or an independent state we do not yet know.

When this settlement was at the height of its prosperity, about 1500 BC, it was destroyed by a disastrous earthquake. The inhabitants, however, had time to leave, taking their valuables with them. Later the city was buried by pumice when the volcano erupted.

The violence of that eruption must have been almost unimaginable. The volcano, after a series of paroxysms, collapsed into itself, creating a huge caldera into which the sea poured, leaving the once round island of Santorini as a mere broken crescent. The amount of

A reconstruction of a wooden bed found at Thera

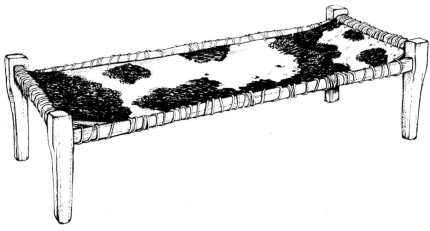

90

These jars in a basement storeroom at Akrotiri were cracked by the red-hot pumice that fell on them.

volcanic tephra produced by the eruption was awe-inspiring—more than a hundred feet deep in places. Drillings on the seabed between Santorini and eastern Crete have revealed traces of extensive tephra deposits there, which means that eastern Crete itself must have been blanketed with poisonous ash. Some scholars believe that the eruption was accompanied by severe earthquakes, or that the formation of the caldera created tidal waves which would have swamped the northern coasts of Crete.

It is little wonder that Marinatos should have associated the destruction of Minoan Crete with the volcano on Santorini. Unfortunately, the archaeological evidence available so far does not square with the opinions of vulcanologists.

The pottery finds on Santorini and on Crete show that the city of Akrotiri was destroyed around 1500 BC, but that the Cretan settlements were not destroyed until a generation later. Archaeologists would like to think that there must therefore have been two eruptions, separated by a gap of twenty-five to fifty years; the first one, around 1500 BC, which buried Akrotiri but seemed to have had little effect on Crete, while a second one around 1450 BC ruined central and eastern Crete by a combination of earthquake followed by fire, tidal waves on the north coast, and volcanic ash fall-out.

At present, however, many vulcanologists insist that there was only the one eruption, and that it probably lasted no longer than a year. There is no evidence of the extensive erosion between ash layers that would have been apparent if there had been a lull of many years in between, nor do they believe that a volcano like Santorini would erupt twice so violently in such a short space of time after lying dormant for thousands of years.

It is a puzzle which can only be solved by the further investigations of archaeologists and vulcanologists working together. The most recent suggestion to emerge is that the earthquake and the eruption were separated by twenty-five to fifty years; soil traces have been found between the earthquake ruins at Akrotiri and the lowest layer of pumice. Perhaps, therefore, the earthquake that shattered the city of Akrotiri was so severe that the whole island of Thera was totally abandoned, and years passed before the devastating eruption of the volcano.

11

Gazi and Karphi: after Knossos

The three centuries between the fall of Knossos in about 1400 BC and the Dorian invasions of about 1100 BC are as yet poorly understood. They are best divided into two phases, covering respectively the fourteenth and thirteenth centuries, and the twelfth century BC.

By 1425 BC people had returned to the depopulated areas of central and eastern Crete, and were living, it seems, under the domination of a Mycenaean king of Knossos. Their towns were rebuilt, but the other palaces were left desolate. Then, in about 1400 BC, the Palace at Knossos was suddenly burnt down at the height of its prosperity, for reasons which we do not yet understand. Some scholars believe that the cause was a revolt of native Cretans against their Mycenaean overlords.

After this there was a noticeable reaction against things Mycenaean, and a return to native Cretan culture ensued. The towns at Knossos, Phaestos, Mallia and Zakro (but not the palaces) returned to normal, as did many other towns; but we do not as yet know a great deal about them. Our best evidence for these two centuries comes from cemeteries rather than from settlements.

The typical tomb was now a chamber approached by a horizontal passage in the hillside and hollowed out of the soft rock, intended only for three or four members of a family. The dead were placed in terracotta coffins made in the shape of clothes chests or bath-tubs, the latter having actually been used as baths before serving their final purpose. They were decorated by the same means and with much the same patterns as the contemporary pottery.

The pottery is represented principally by goblets and stirrup-jars of all shapes and sizes for storing liquids. The patterns are mostly

A chamber tomb cut into the soft rock at Knossos in about 1300 BC with an intact coffin inside.

simplifications of the favourite motifs of fifteenth-century pottery.

Terracotta figures are now common in shrines and tombs. Typical is a goddess standing with her hands raised. A hollow wheel-made tube forms her skirt, and the upper part of her body, also basically wheel-made, is modelled into human shape. These figures have a primitive, even ugly, appearance, and show how standards had gone down since the Snake Goddesses of the seventeenth century BC. Jewellery is now rare, and seals revert to their Pre-palatial simplicity, being made of soft and easily worked stones such as steatite in place of the harder and more decorative quartzes.

In about 1200 BC the island was settled peacefully by newcomers from Mycenaean Greece, refugees from serious troubles in their

94

A terracotta goddess, about two feet six inches tall, crowned with poppies, from a house-shrine at Gazi.

homeland, for all the principal Mycenaean towns and palaces had been burnt down—we do not yet know by whom.

A new society grew up based on a joint Minoan-Mycenaean culture. We can see the beginning of a return to prosperity and a more settled way of life, but everything ended about 1100 BC when members of the Dorian branch of the Greek family invaded Crete in great numbers and brought the Bronze Age to an end.

Two twelfth-century sites are of particular interest for the light they throw on this late period. The first is Gazi, a few miles west of Knossos, where a house was accidentally discovered in 1936. Peasants had come upon two terracotta figures of goddesses like those described above. When news reached the authorities, Spiridon Marinatos conducted a small-scale excavation; more was not possible

95

as the site was in the middle of a vineyard. He found a rectangular room, evidently a house-shrine, and in it three more terracotta goddesses, and some scraps of pottery. The five goddesses are some of the finest of their kind. One in particular is worthy of note, for she wears a crown of poppies, the heads of which are slashed as if to extract opium. She may have been a goddess of drug-induced peace and forgetfulness.

The second site is the settlement at Karphi, situated some twenty miles south-east of Knossos and over 4,000 feet above sea-level. It was discovered by Arthur Evans in 1896, but was left until John Pendlebury excavated it in 1938–9. It was the last thing he did, for two years later he was to die heroically fighting for his beloved Crete against yet another barbarian invasion. In his excavation report he notes that his workmen included two Albanian murderers, a sheep-stealer from Mount Ida and an alleged leper from Cyprus.

The settlement lasted from about 1150 to 1050 BC, and was then quietly deserted. It thus has one foot in the Bronze Age and one in the Iron Age.

Although very poor—only two seal-stones were found, and no gold or silver at all—Karphi boasted two important buildings, the 'Big House' and the Temple. The 'Big House' was large and complicated, with a Mycenaean type of megaron, which consists of a great hall with three parts: porch, vestibule and throne room. The Temple had an altar and a ledge on which had been placed nine terracotta goddesses like those from Gazi. There was also a Priest's House, leading out of the Temple.

Like a modern Greek town, Karphi had a main square, paved streets, a bazaar area, and stone houses with flat roofs. The inhabitants buried their dead in beehive tombs, a sort of poor man's version of the royal tombs of Mycenae.

The best kind of pottery in the twelfth century is decorated in the so-called Fringed and Octopus styles. The Fringed style is based on thick graceful curves with fringed borders, while between the curves are delicate secondary patterns of fine lines. Out of this grew the Octopus style, in which the central ornament is now a gracefully writhing octopus, between whose ribbon-like tentacles are finely drawn sketches of birds, fish, and animals.

This twelfth-century BC culture, composed of many of the best of Minoan and Mycenaean elements, might well have continued and developed. But it was not to be. The invasion of the Dorian Greeks put a sudden end to the Minoan way of life.

The Octopus style

96

12

Sacred Caves

As it is mostly made of limestone, Crete is honeycombed with caves, many of them very large and very elaborate. The early Cretans, who had no temples, preferred to worship their gods and goddesses either in palace-shrines or in caves, especially when the caves were situated near the tops of mountains. We do not know why this should have been so. One reason may well be the stalactites in the caves, which they regarded as particularly holy; another, the mysterious atmosphere of a cave. Here they would leave their offerings: vases and figures of terracotta or bronze, jewellery, or weapons, according to the nature of the god or goddess or their own personal preference.

Such sacred caves have been explored intermittently and sometimes scientifically excavated since the 1880s, but no systematic survey of all Cretan caves was undertaken until after the Second World War, when the French archaeologist and explorer Paul Faure made a thorough investigation of them.

Five caves are of particular interest for the light they throw on Minoan religion. The first is the Kamares Cave, high up on the southern slopes of Mount Ida, which was accidentally discovered by a shepherd in the early 1890s near the modern village of Kamares. He found in it some two dozen vases with brightly coloured designs painted on a black background, which he sold to the Museum of Heraklion, where they were christened Kamares ware. The cave was properly excavated by the British School at Athens in 1913, and more pottery of the same kind was found.

It is evident that this cave served as a holy place for the inhabitants of the first palace of Phaestos, from where its enormous arched

97

Bronze statuette of a male worshipper from the Psychro Cave.

entrance can easily be seen on a clear day. Unlike most Cretan sacred caves its useful life was short, as it did not survive the fall of the early palace as a cult place. Possibly it was damaged in some way by the earthquake which destroyed that palace, and so the faithful took their offerings elsewhere.

Next is the Idaean Cave, high up on the eastern slopes of the same Mount Ida. In historical times it was the most celebrated of all Cretan caves, for it was here that the great god Zeus was principally worshipped, and it was one of the Cretan caves identified as his birthplace. It consisted of an enormous grotto, about ninety feet wide and thirty feet high, with a smaller grotto leading out of it. It, too, was accidentally discovered by a shepherd, in 1884. He found a number of antiquities in it and told the glad news to his friends in the village, who began to plunder the cave. The archaeologist Joseph Hazzidakis hurried to the spot when he heard of this, and tried to stop the wholesale looting. He did not meet with much success at first, but in the end, in August 1885, he arranged for a proper excavation to be made. A vast quantity of objects was found, especially bronzes, most of them of the eighth century BC.

So far nothing Minoan had turned up, but the excavation was far from complete. In 1956 Spiridon Marinatos conducted a supplementary investigation with a view to a complete excavation. This did not happen, but in a short time he had found fragments of Minoan pottery at least as early as 1400 BC. There is still much to do, but it can now be said that the cave was in use in Minoan times and continued in regular use down to the sixth century BC.

At Arkalochori some twelve miles south of Knossos, peasants had for years been ransacking a small cave for bronze weapons to sell as scrap, when in 1912 Hazzidakis decided to excavate it. He found more bronze weapons and some pottery, but stopped at a fall of rock which he mistook for the end of the cave. Here the matter rested until 1934, when some children found a number of bronzes and a miniature gold double axe, brought to light by badgers at the mouth of the cave. The villagers promptly searched the cave and found a rich deposit of gold and bronze offerings beyond the rockfall. Marinatos then stepped in. He cleared the cave in two seasons and found a treasure of sacred double axes, a hundred in bronze, six in silver and twenty-six in gold. Many were delicately incised and some had Cretan writing engraved on them. He also found a number of enormous bronze swords, some nearly six feet long.

These discoveries made the Arkalochori Cave the richest of all so far explored in Crete. It would seem that it was in use as a sanctuary from about 2000 BC down to about 1450 BC, when an earthquake caused the roof to fall in; offerings were then deposited in front of the entrance until about 1100 BC, when they ceased.

Who was the warlike deity to whom these offerings were made? Possibly Zeus, possibly Athena herself, for we know she was worshipped at Knossos around 1400 BC.

The fourth cave to be considered is situated near Psychro, about ten miles east of Arkalochori. It has been claimed, but probably without justification, as the famous Dictaean Cave of classical times, where, according to the legend, the god Zeus was born and brought up in secret by his mother, for his father Kronos had the habit of eating all his offspring to prevent any of his sons growing up to dethrone him as the supreme deity. Here, too, Minos, like Moses, was said to have found the Laws.

The Psychro Cave was accidentally discovered by peasants in 1883, and was explored by Halbherr and Hazzidakis two years later. In 1894 and 1895 Arthur Evans visited the cave and bought a number of bronzes from the inhabitants, and in 1896 he made a small excavation, finding animal bones, pottery and more bronzes. Finally, in 1900, the cave was thoroughly excavated by D. G. Hogarth. It was like no excavation before or since.

Bronze statuette of a female worshipper from the Psychro Cave.

The enormous cave was composed of an upper and a lower grotto. Much of the former was obstructed by enormous boulders which had fallen from the roof; these Hogarth broke up with dynamite. The finds, which included an altar, were interesting, but not particularly spectacular.

The lower grotto had more to offer. It was full of stalactites, in the crevices of which many bronze objects had been wedged: dagger blades, votive double axes, fibulae (safety-pins), and statuettes. In many cases the stalactites had actually closed over the bronzes, and had to be chipped away. In Hogarth's words: 'In the hope of the reward, which I gave for the better objects, and in the excitement of so curious a search, which, in their earlier illicit diggings it had not occurred to them to attempt, the villagers, both men and women, worked with frantic energy, clinging singly to the pillars high above the subterranean lake, or grouping half a dozen flaring lights over a productive patch of mud at the water's edge. It was a grotesque sight, without precedent in an archaeologist's experience.'

In all, the expedition recovered some five hundred bronzes and objects in gold, lead, precious stone, ivory, bone, and terracotta.

99

Miniature gold axes from the cave at Arkalochori.

The cave seems to have come into use when the Kamares Cave was deserted, in about 1700 BC and to have continued without a break down to the sixth century BC, with a brief revival of interest in the Roman period.

We finish with a cave at Amnisos, the ancient harbour of Knossos, which survived into classical times as a sanctuary of Eileithyia, goddess of childbirth. We may assume that the original goddess of this place exercised the same functions, and almost certainly had the same name, for it is found in a Cretan inscribed tablet from Knossos of about 1400 BC. In 1886 Hazzidakis and Halbherr excavated this cave and identified it correctly. Their claim was contested at the time, but further excavations by Marinatos in 1929 entirely confirmed it.

The cave is about a hundred and eighty feet long by thirty feet wide, and only about eight feet high. In the middle was the Holy of Holies, a cylindrical stalactite enclosed by a low rectangular wall. Offerings seem to have started about 1400 BC, and to have reached their maximum in the ninth and eighth centuries BC. In the third century BC there was a revival of interest which lasted until the fifth century AD.

The only offerings actually found in this cave consist of pottery, but other objects, especially clothing—a popular offering in classical times to goddesses of childbirth—may well have been dedicated, and if so, would have perished completely.

These are only the five most interesting of the Minoan sacred caves, but many more have been identified, thanks to the adventurous and scholarly spirit of Paul Faure. And there is always the chance that one day, in a land as full of caves as Crete, another even richer one will come to light.

The Cave of Eileithyia.

101

13

Cretan Writing: the Decipherment of Linear B

Writing in Crete is a puzzle which has not yet been completely solved. Three different scripts were employed at various times in Minoan Crete—or four, if the tantalising and unique Phaestos Disc is included. The earliest, the so-called Hieroglyphic script, was in use from 2000 to 1600 BC. It consisted of pictorial signs representing common objects, such as a head, a hand, a leg, a fish, a star, a double axe, and so on; rather like Egyptian hieroglyphs. The signs are mostly found engraved on seal-stones, but were also inscribed on clay tablets. They have not been deciphered, and, in the present state of our knowledge, are not likely to be.

Two closely related linear scripts arose, by a process of simplification, out of the Hieroglyphic: that is to say, the picture-signs were written faster and more simply, so that the pictures became squiggles. The earliest, known as Linear A, was used between about 1900 BC and the fall of the palaces around 1450 BC. It is most commonly found inscribed on clay tablets, especially at Knossos, Ayia Triada and Zakro, but it may well be that most of the writing was done in ink on papyrus, which would not have survived the Cretan climate. There were about seventy-five signs and a number of ideograms to indicate certain objects pictorially as an additional guide to the reader. A set of a hundred and fifty tablets from Ayia Triada can be seen from the ideograms to be concerned with agricultural produce.

This script has not been deciphered. Although scholars are working on it, success is unlikely until many more tablets are excavated somewhere. However, two conclusions can be drawn: the signs must denote syllables; and, whatever the language is, it is not Greek.

The second of the scripts, Linear B, is of much greater importance, because we can now read it. It was in use at Knossos in the last days of the Palace, between 1450 and 1400 BC. It is not found elsewhere in Crete, but it is recorded in the Mycenaean palaces of Greece between 1400 and 1200 BC. This script is not a development of Linear A, but derives independently from Hieroglyphic. It consists of 87 signs, and a number of ideograms closely related to those of Linear A.

The tablets on which the script is inscribed are flat slabs of clay. Many are about five inches across by two inches tall, but some are more the shape of a page, about five inches across by nine inches tall. The signs were inscribed with a stylus on the hard, but unfired, clay. The tablets were never deliberately fired but were used only for day-to-day needs and were pulped when they had served their purpose. As they were not intentionally fired, they have only survived when they were accidentally involved in a fire, which 'cooked' them. As with Linear A it may well be that more permanent records were written in ink on papyrus which has not survived.

But why did the Cretans write on wet clay when they could use papyrus? There are two possible answers. First, papyrus had to be imported from Egypt and was expensive, while clay was cheap. Second, in store-rooms, and that is where most of the tablets seem to have been used, mice or silver-fish would eat papyrus, as they are liable to eat paper labels in Cretan museum store-rooms today.

Evans found about four thousand Linear B tablets in the Palace at Knossos in the debris of the final destruction of about 1400 BC. Although many of the tablets were found in the early years of the excavations, very few were made available for study until after Evans's death in 1941.

After the Second World War the Knossos tablets were at last published, together with about six hundred in the same script which had been found in 1939 by the American archaeologist Carl Blegen at Pylos in South Greece. The stage was now set for decipherment.

One of the scholars who set to work was a young English architect

Bronze double axe inscribed with two characters of the Linear A script.

103

Linear B script.

by the name of Michael Ventris. As a boy in 1936 he had visited an exhibition in London to celebrate the fiftieth anniversary of the British School at Athens. Here he had heard Sir Arthur Evans lecture about his discoveries at Knossos and the mysterious Cretan writing, and was inspired then and there with the ambition to decipher it. He never lost interest in the subject, and in 1952 he announced that he had indeed deciphered the Linear B script. It was Greek, he claimed; although Greek in a primitive form.

To decipher a strange script you normally require a bilingual; that is to say, a document which gives the same information in a known language as well as in the script to be deciphered. The Rosetta Stone is such a bilingual, and it led to the decipherment of Egyptian hieroglyphics.

Ventris had no bilingual. He merely had an unusually brilliant intellect and an acquaintance with wartime code-breaking methods, which involved a detailed analysis of the frequency and relative position of every sign.

There were too few signs for Linear B to be picture-writing, too many for an alphabet, so it had to be a syllabary, as was the related Cypriot script which had long ago been deciphered. By a process of trial and error, and by matching the results with the ideograms, Ventris eventually worked out a set of values for the signs which made sense as Greek.

There were difficulties, because the script was not really suitable for Greek, having evidently been devised originally for some other language. The signs stood either for a vowel or for a consonant-plus-vowel. Ventris was therefore often obliged to insert an unnecessary vowel where two consonants came together, or to omit a final consonant. Thus on a tablet with an ideogram for 'footstool', for which the Greek is *thranus*, the word in Linear B became *ta-ra-nu*.

When Ventris's decipherment appeared in the *Journal of Hellenic Studies* in 1953, there were many who were at once persuaded, but some who doubted. Most of the doubts were, however, laid to rest

104

Michael Ventris.

when Blegen published a tablet from Pylos which Ventris could not have seen when he was working out his decipherment. In this tablet were ideograms for a tripod-cauldron, and for various kinds of jar, all correctly described in Greek when read by Ventris's system.

What can the Knossos tablets tell of Minoan Crete? Their contents, at first reading, are rather disappointing, consisting, as the ideograms suggest, for the most part of lists of dedications, palace stores, armaments and agricultural produce. Dedications to gods and goddesses, however, are of considerable interest when we recognise old friends from much later times such as Zeus, Hera, Poseidon, Hermes, Athena, Artemis, and Eleuthia (later, Eileithyia), the goddess of the sacred cave at Amnisos.

The tripod tablet from Pylos

It would be too much to expect any form of literature on these tablets; they are simply administrative crumbs from the rich man's table. But perhaps the most important thing to be learned from them is that there were true Greeks at Knossos as early as 1400 BC, and on the Greek mainland probably very much earlier.

One day someone may well discover, perhaps in Egypt, a papyrus containing a work of literature in Linear B, and we will then learn whether our guesses and deductions about Minoan Crete are very wide of the mark. Perhaps this book will then have to be re-written. Perhaps not.

No.		Value	No.		Value	No.		Value
01		da	30		ni	59		ta
02		ro	31		sa	60		ra
03		pa	32		qo	61		o
04		te	33		ra_3	62		pte
05		to	34			63		
06		na	35			64		
07		di	36		jo	65		ju
08		a	37		ti	66		ta_2
09		se	38		e	67		ki
10		u	39		pi	68		ro_2
11		po	40		wi	69		tu
12		so	41		si	70		ko
13		me	42		wo	71		
14		do	43		ai	72		pe
15		mo	44		ke	73		mi
16		pa_2	45		de	74		ze
17		za	46		je	75		we
18			47			76		ra_2
19			48		nwa	77		ka
20		zo	49			78		qe
21		qi	50		pu	79		zu
22			51		du	80		ma
23		mu	52		no	81		ku
24		ne	53		ri	82		
25		a_2	54		wa	83		
26		ru	55		nu	84		
27		re	56		pa_3	85		
28		i	57		ja	86		
29		pu_2	58		su	87		

The Linear B script
and its values

107

EPILOGUE

Much has been achieved in Minoan archaeology in only three-quarters of a century. Much, too, remains to be done. The following are some of the problems which remain outstanding.

Are there any more palaces waiting to be discovered? Almost certainly the answer to this is, yes. In the last few years Greek archaeologists have been excavating a prosperous settlement in West Crete, in the middle of the modern city of Canea. Occupation started about 4000 BC, and continued till the end of the Minoan era, about 1100 BC. The finds to date include much fine pottery of First-palatial and Second-palatial types, and the excavators suspect the presence of a palace nearby.

What was the cause of the widespread destructions throughout East and Central Crete about 1450 BC? Was it earthquake, shock waves or enemy action? And did West Crete share in these destructions? At the moment very little excavation of Minoan sites has been done in West Crete, but the current excavation at Canea and possibly other sites may answer this question.

What was happening in Crete between 1400 and 1100 BC? And why, although most of the towns were reoccupied after the destructions of 1450 BC, were none of the palaces occupied again as palaces? The answers to these questions will surely be found when the right sites are discovered and excavated.

What is the language of the Hieroglyphic and Linear A scripts? The decipherment of Linear A could well follow on from the discovery of many more Linear A tablets, but unless that happens it is unlikely that anything will be achieved. Only when Linear A can be read will the decipherment of Hieroglyphic follow suit. When this is done, we will know who the Minoans really were, what language they spoke and what gods they worshipped.

BOOKS FOR FURTHER READING

CHADWICK, J., The Decipherment of Linear B (Cambridge University Press, 1958)

EVANS, A. J., The Palace of Minos at Knossos (Macmillan, London 1921–35)

EVANS, JOAN, Time and Chance. The Story of Arthur Evans and his Forbears (Longman Group, London 1943)

HIGGINS, REYNOLD, Minoan and Mycenaean Art (Thames & Hudson, London 1967)

The Greek Bronze Age (British Museum, London 1970)

HOOD, SINCLAIR, The Home of the Heroes (Thames & Hudson, London 1967)

The Minoans (Thames & Hudson, London 1971)

HUTCHINSON, R. W., Prehistoric Crete (Penguin Books, Harmondsworth 1962)

MARINATOS, S. N. and HIRMER, M., Crete and Mycenae (Thames & Hudson, London 1960)

PENDLEBURY, J. D. S., The Archaeology of Crete (Methuen, London 1939, reprinted)

VENTRIS, M. and CHADWICK, J., Documents in Mycenaean Greek (Cambridge University Press 1956)

INDEX